In Search of Peace

Discovering God's Plan for Happiness and Hope

Margarita C. Treviño, Ph.D.

Woman's Missionary Union, SBC
Birmingham, Alabama

Woman's Missionary Union
P. O. Box 830010
Birmingham, AL 35283-0010

© 1999 by Woman's Missionary Union
All rights reserved. First printing 1999
Printed in the United States of America
Woman's Missionary Union® and WMU® are registered
   trademarks.

Dewey Decimal Classification: 155.9
Subject Headings: STRESS (PSYCHOLOGY)
                    MENTAL HEALTH
                    SPIRITUAL LIFE

Unless otherwise indicated, all Scripture quotations are from
Contemporary English Version, © American Bible Society, 1995.
Used by permission.

Cover design by Say Saysombath

ISBN: 1-56309-302-2
L994112•0199•1M1

Dedication

*To my parents
José and Ysaura Sánchez
from whom I learned
the significance of
unconditional love*

Acknowledgments

I am deeply grateful to:

my husband, Hugo, for his unwavering encouragement and support of my work;

my children, Nina and Hugo II, for their love;

the countless men and women here and abroad who have enriched my life through their participation in my stress management seminars;

dear friends and colleagues who have been sources of encouragement and instruction for me along the way;

Elizabeth Rivera for her encouragement for me to write this book;

Carole Fite for her editorial contributions and tireless assistance in the production of this work.

CONTENTS

Foreword vii

Introduction viii

Chapter 1: What Stress Is 1
Where stress comes from ...everywhere! 1
The economic impact of stress 6
The spiritual gateway to stress management 7
How we respond to stress 8
Walking the tightrope 9
How stress presents itself 11
Personal Stress Awareness Inventory 11
Two choices 14

Chapter 2: The Importance of Perception 15
Basic concepts about stress 19
Checking your personal level of stress 20

Chapter 3: Responses to Stress 23
Psychological/emotional responses 23
Physical signs and symptoms 24
Spiritual signs and symptoms 25
Take a look at your medicine cabinet 26

Chapter 4: Keys for Managing Stress 29
   **Key 1: Take inventory of stress factors
      in your life today** 29
      Five questions 33
      Spiritual markers for taking inventory
         of stress 34
      Psalm 23 36
   Key 2: Listen to your body 41
      Stage One: The alarm stage 41
      Stage Two: The resistance stage 42
      Stage Three: The exhaustion stage 44
      Listening to your body 44
      Spiritual markers for listening to your body . . .46

(continued)

Key 3: **Maintain a balanced lifestyle** 48
    What a balanced lifestyle is not 48
    Contributing factors to a state of
        disequilibrium 48
    Characteristics of a balanced lifestyle 49
    Steps to a balanced lifestyle 50
    There is hope for the family 53

Chapter 5: The Vital Signs of a Healthy Family 55
A healthy family 55
Handles for daily living 57
Handle with care 60
Commitment of love 61

Chapter 6: Establishing a Balanced Lifestyle 63
Spiritual markers for taking inventory of the balance in
    your lifestyle 64
Pulling it all together 65
Meditation on God's Word as a technique for
    managing stress 68
Other suggestions 69
You will never stumble 70
The choice is yours 70

Chapter 7: Looking Back to the Future 71

Appendix 1: My Personal Plan 79

Appendix 2: The Ultimate Benefit 80

Appendix 3: The Builder 81

Notes 83

Study Guide 85

Foreword

Years ago a furloughing missionary and I were walking from my study to the Family Life Center of our church when he said to me, "I wish I could be as cool and relaxed as you are." Little did he know, but at that very moment I was so uptight I would have twanged in a strong breeze. I just covered it up well.

Stress is one of the common denominators of life. No one can eliminate it all together all the time. It's simply a part of life. Somehow we must learn to manage it or it will manage us. That's why this book by Margarita Treviño is so valuable—valuable to me personally and of value to you. It scratches where we itch, touches where we live, speaks to a need we all have.

Margarita is eminently qualified to write on this subject by both training and experience. She knows her subject and her subjects. In a uniquely succinct and practical way, she helps us to see that we have three choices with stress: flight! fright! or fight!

As she discusses both its causes and how to cope with it, she presents a wonderful blend of both practical application and eternal truth as they relate to stress. She covers stress in all the areas of life—family, finance, workplace, technological advances, as well as the challenge to evangelize the world. This not just another book on stress, of which there are many. It is a book from a biblical and spiritual perspective as well as from the physical.

When I started reading the manuscript I intended to tell you what my favorite chapter was. But I kept changing with each new chapter I read. I finally decided I liked them all. So will you.

Margarita closes with a page entitled, "My Personal Plan," to encourage you to write down specific actions and goals that you will take to manage stress more effectively in your life. What better way to end than that?

While this is Margarita's first book, I predict it will not be her last. When you have read her works, you will agree that anything she touches has quality written all over it. Read on and you will see for yourself.

—Paul W. Powell,
former president, Annuity Board
of the Southern Baptist Convention

Introduction

Stress has become known as an inevitable enemy of modern-day society. We have become so accustomed to the idea of being overextended, exhausted, and frustrated that if we aren't experiencing these feelings, we wonder if we're okay. While we have gained mastery over many scientific and technological advancements, human nature remains unchanged. We are responsible for how we deal with stress. Since the norm of the day is rapid change and the need to continually adapt to our surroundings, we are at risk of becoming victims to the hurried and overloading demands of daily living.

Stress, however, can be a benefit for us. It can serve as a barometer to help us gauge our ability to manage the requirements of daily living. It can keep us in check regarding the balance in our lifestyle. It can give us direction for making positive changes. If we heed the call to take hold of a spiritual approach to managing stress, stress becomes an asset instead of a liability. Stress that is placed in a spiritual perspective, coupled with mental, emotional, and physical considerations, provides a firm foundation for the celebration of life.

This book is about understanding what stress is, how it affects us, and what we can do to harness this energy for successful living. It is my desire to help you discover God's plan for happiness, hope, and peace as you deal with trials in your life.

1
What Stress Is

Stress means different things to different people. Over the years, I have asked hundreds of people to define stress. Responses vary. Some of the most common answers define stress as *having a tight feeling, nervousness, being irritable, being unable to sleep, forgetfulness,* or *being under a lot of pressure.*

These answers describe *symptoms* of stress. Stress is the body's nonspecific response to a stimulus, a demand.[1] The stimulus can be internal, as in the case of a toothache, a stomach pain, or a headache. Or it can be external, as in anything that's in our environment. An external stimulus could be a telephone call, a disappointment, an argument, a birthday party, a job promotion, or taking a vacation. An external stimulus is anything that requires a response from us.

Stress is associated not only with difficult and painful circumstances (known as *distress).* We experience stress when we are happy and having a good time, as well (known as *eustress).*[2] The impact of stress on the individual is the same. Regardless of the reason for the stress, the body's responses affect us in the same manner. We experience the *flight-or-fight response*. We decide either to run away from the situation or to face the situation and deal with it.

Stress is a universal human experience. It doesn't know cultural boundaries. It is not limited by ethnicity, age, gender, residence, or social status. Stress affects all living persons. As long as we are in this life on earth, we will experience stress.

**Where stress comes from ...
everywhere!**

- We deal with stress in the course of providing for our basic needs, such as food, clothing, and shelter. These needs are essential for our physical survival.

- We also have mental and emotional needs. These also are important to our survival. We have the need to feel loved and accepted. These feelings enable us to develop a sense of belonging and to have a positive sense of self-worth.

- Communications and relationships are basic to our survival. We were made to need other people in our lives. The Bible says, "men and women need each other. . . . God is the one who created everything" (1 Corinthians 11:11-12). "Everything comes from the Lord. All things were made because of him and will return to him" (Romans 11:36). Thomas Merton wrote, ". . . the truth remains that our destiny is to love one another as Christ has loved us."[3]

Our needs, relationships, and experiences make demands on us and produce stress. To these we could add other dimensions of personal needs such as choosing a mate and choosing our lifework. We have decisions to make about finances, employment, and education. Meeting our health care needs is another major source of stress. Many individuals cannot afford health care insurance. In some cases this means postponing medical care or not getting medical care at all. Securing transportation is another major source of stress, whether we drive, take public transportation, or use car pools.

As we consider our total makeup, we recognize that we also have spiritual needs. The Apostle Paul wrote, "Everyone who is ruled by the Holy Spirit thinks about spiritual thins. If our minds are ruled by our desires, we will die. But if our minds are ruled by the Spirit, we will have life and peace" (Romans 8:5*b*-6). Becoming aware of our spirituality can be stressful. We have to make long-term choices, and that's not always easy to do.

On Christian behavior, the Apostle Paul wrote:

> "Be sincere in your love for others. Hate everything that is evil and hold tight to everything that is good. Love each other as brothers and sisters and honor others more than you do yourself. Never give up. Eagerly follow the Holy Sprit and serve the Lord. Let your hope make you glad. Be patient in time of trouble and never stop praying. Take care of God's needy

What Stress Is

people and welcome strangers into your home. "Ask God to bless everyone who mistreats you. Ask him to bless them and not to curse them. When others are happy, be happy with them, and when they are sad, be sad. Be friendly with everyone. Don't be proud and feel that you are smarter than others. Make friends with ordinary people. Don't mistreat someone who has mistreated you. But try to earn the respect of others, and do your best to live at peace with everyone.

"Dear friends, don't try to get even. Let God take revenge. In the Scriptures the Lord says, 'I am the one to take revenge and pay them back.' The Scriptures also say, 'If your enemies are hungry, give them something to eat. And if they are thirsty, give them something to drink. This will be the same as piling burning coals on their heads.' Don't let evil defeat you, but defeat evil with good" (Romans 12:9-21).

Family is another significant source of stress-producing experiences. The family, too, concerns itself with basic survival needs, such as food, clothing, and shelter. This requires financial resources. To have financial resources, the family must have a means of income. To have income, there must be work. The type of work the family has will depend on the type of education or training family members have and the availability of employment opportunities.

As the family evolves, so do the sources of stress. When the children are young, there are needs to provide child care and education and to see them grow into independent adults. However, the needs and problems don't stop with adulthood. As children marry and form their own families, the needs and problems of the extended family become part of the needs and problems of the whole family. In so many cases, the older parents or grandparents share heartaches and frustrations about their sons or daughters or grandchildren. Problems related to failing marriages, unemployment, health challenges, juvenile delinquency, and others cross family boundaries. Child care, transportation, environmental safety, and protection from crime are all sources of stress.

As individuals make decisions about their spiritual needs, so do families: "My family and I are going to worship and obey the LORD" (Joshua 24:15*b*). Some families decide that their spiritual needs matter; others decide that they don't. Family lifestyles reveal their choices.

Family dynamics also include communication and relationships. As developmental needs of family units, these areas can also cause stress. The family system in which we are raised determines to a large extent how we learn to communicate and develop relationships with the outside world. The home serves as a safety net to learn these skills or, on the contrary, it can be a minefield of insult and painful experiences. Both outcomes produce stress.

Some people may see stress in the community-at-large as something distant to them. Unless we are affected directly, there is a tendency to dismiss the impact of stressful situations as being "somebody else's problems." But whether there is a direct or indirect connection, we are all affected by stressors in our communities. The economy, education, employment, and public and environmental safety are different forms of community-based stress. Housing, transportation resources, and even access to health care services are some of the challenges that communities face. The political system and the religions present in a community also affect the overall quality of life.

It's great when whole communities gather to celebrate the Fourth of July or when a new business comes to town and creates much-needed jobs. Yet, these are stressful situations, too. A community can also be taken hostage by uncontrolled violence and crime, homelessness and poverty, and racial tensions. A total community may be under heavy stress when it experiences a natural disaster. All of these conditions, the happy and the difficult, are sources of stress in communities.

A common stressor around the world is war or the threat of war. International terrorism, governments in transition, world hunger, peace talks, unabated disease conditions, and the fear of global warming are all sources of stress.

As with the other types of stress, not all worldwide stress is negative. Christians use the concern for world evangelization *positively* by reaching out in many ways to spread the Gospel. We also celebrate with world-class athletes, Nobel Prize winners, and others who contribute to the global quality of life. We don't

What Stress Is

complain when, with the touch of a button, we can see what is happening around the world, although the information may be depressing. We enjoy the ability to surf the Internet. Technological advances are an ever-growing source of stress, particularly in industrialized nations.

We are part of a global society bombarded with stress from multiple sources. Not only are we under the influence of various sources of stress, but the bombardment is *constant*. In most cases, it is also *negative*. Notice the newspaper headlines and television news reports. Listen to radio newscasts. These media sources highlight conflict, social disorder, and various types of losses from economic to reputations, among other factors. If there's an element of suspense or sensationalism, the public is more likely to consume the information. These are all negative forms of stressors.

If you view an evening news report, be it local, national, or international, chances are your blood pressure will be more elevated after the newscast than it was before. It doesn't matter whether or not the information affects you directly, the news report will affect you just the same.

I visited with a young man attending one of my conferences on stress. "I'm tired and not in a very good mood when I get home from work," he said. When I asked him what he did to unwind when he arrived home from work, he said, "I go to the bedroom, close the door, and listen to the evening news. By dinnertime, I don't feel like being around my wife or my kids. It's really bad." He identified a major part of the problem. Instead of relaxing, he was compounding the burden of stress by adding more negative information. Stress has a cumulative effect, and this young father was having stress overload.

Sometimes we may think that we are "relaxing," when in reality we are adding even more stressors to our minds and bodies when we're already tired. No wonder we find it hard to function in harmony with those around us.

Gauge your capacity to absorb information, positive or negative. The next time you feel *out of control* and you can't quite put your finger on why you feel that way, ask yourself if you have been consuming an overload of information, especially if it's negative information. Then think of ways to reduce the amount of information you receive on a daily basis. Perhaps you can take a walk in a park or seek solitude in a quiet place. You can be alone without being lonely. Being comfortable in our aloneness can help to replenish our mind, body, and spirit. It empowers us to reach out beyound ourselves to others. Perhaps you prefer being around people. If you are feeling overwhelmed, seek the companionship of those who complement your need for quiet time. Imagine not feeling that you have to be talking to be engaged in a meaningful relationship! Instead of gazing at the television set, hold the hand of a loved one and allow the power of presence to yield peace and serenity. Setting aside quiet time—distancing yourself from the television, radio, and telephones—can help limit the impact of information bombardment. It allows you to maintain a sense of balance.

The awareness of feeling out of control has served as a way to help me determine how much information I can handle, particularly if the information is negative. I simply set limits. Sometimes I'll go days and weeks without tuning in to news reports, reading the newspaper, or listening to the radio. This simple action helps me control stress instead of allowing stress to rob me of positive energy that I can invest productively elsewhere.

The economic impact of stress
Stress is expensive. Recent studies indicate that "Up to 90% of all visits to primary care physicians are for stress-related complaints."[4]

Research continues to confirm the role of stress in a series of disease conditions, including cardiovascular disease, cancer, gastrointestinal disorders, and a variety of other disorders associated with disturbances of the immune system.

Other costs of stress are seen in the statistics on the next page.

What Stress Is

- Up to 80% of industrial accidents are due to stress.
- Over 50% of lost work days are stress-related.
- 14% of all workers say stress caused them to quit or change jobs in the previous two years.
- Worker's compensation awards for job stress threaten to bankrupt the system in some states.
- Stress on or off the job costs U.S. workplaces an estimated $200 billion a year in reduced productivity, accidents, compensation claims, turnover, health insurance, and medical expenses. This is more than the after-tax profits of the Fortune 500 companies, and 10 times the cost of all strikes combined.[5]

Just think how much wealthier and healthier we would be if we learned to limit our stress and if we responded to stress in a better way!

The spiritual gateway to stress management
This book emphasizes the spiritual gateway to manage stress. There is much information available about what to do physically and mentally to manage stress, and these approaches to managing stress are helpful. The spiritual approach to stress management is not seen as often. I want to emphasize the importance of the spiritual approach. The Bible is full of "how-to's" to deal with stress, and I believe that Jesus Christ is the best role model for managing stress. My prayer is that as you read this book, you'll discover new insights, expand your understanding, or reinforce what you already know about the dynamics of the Christian approach to managing stress. There's a smart way to deal with stress in daily living. It's the Christian way.

How we respond to stress
We respond to stress mentally, emotionally, physically, and spiritually. We respond with our *total being*: mind, body, and spirit. The source of stress may be more centered in one of these areas than others, but the *response* involves all of our being. The illustration below shows the constant interplay between our mental, emotional, physical, and spiritual makeup.

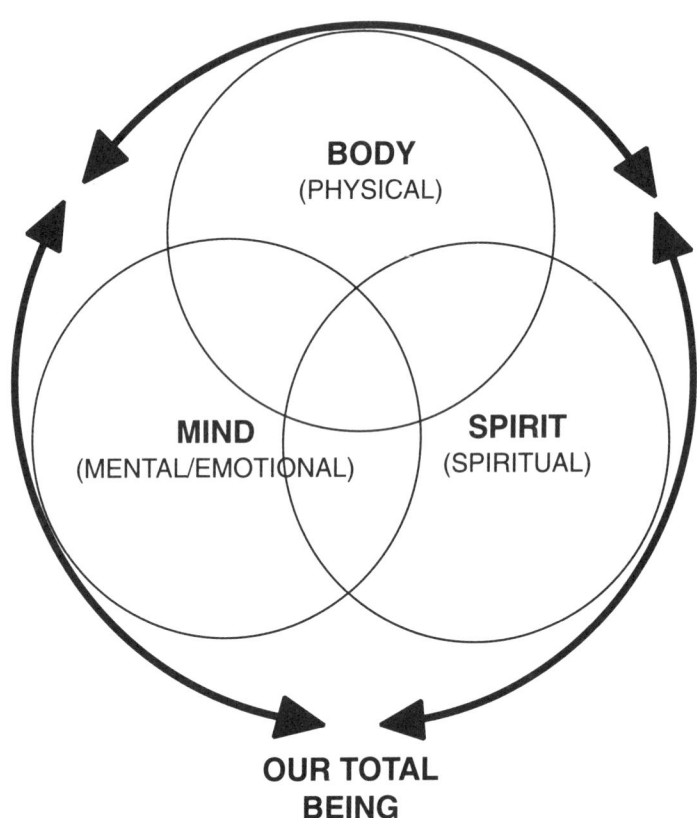

If we hurt in one area, it affects the others. For example, if we have a toothache, chances are we don't feel like being sociable. We prefer to take care of the toothache first, and then perhaps we may feel like being sociable. Or we may have a mental burden that affects the way we feel physically. The same is true of our spiritual nature. We may experience a spiritual dilemma that affects us mentally, emotionally, and physically. Similarly, if we are happy, we feel good all over. Our total makeup as individuals is interwoven, interactive, and interdependent. It's one of the wonders of our creation in God's image.

The psalmist wrote: "You are the one who put me together inside my mother's body, and I praise you because of the wonderful way you created me. Everything you do is marvelous! Of this I have no doubt" (Psalm 139:13-14).

Walking the tightrope
Most of us have watched a trapeze artist walk the tightrope. The artist has to balance one foot at a time to maintain equilibrium and not fall off the rope. You and I do the same thing in our daily walk. Every day, every moment of the day, we seek to maintain an equilibrium, a balance in our lives. Sometimes we do this consciously. Sometimes we do it unconsciously. We do this by making certain choices and taking certain actions. This is how we respond to stress. It's like walking a tightrope.

We can lose our balance in life when we have too much stress. We can also lose our balance in life when we don't have enough stress to engage our minds and our energies. We lose our sense of balance at either extreme. How, then, do we stay balanced, and how do we know if we're in danger of losing our balance?

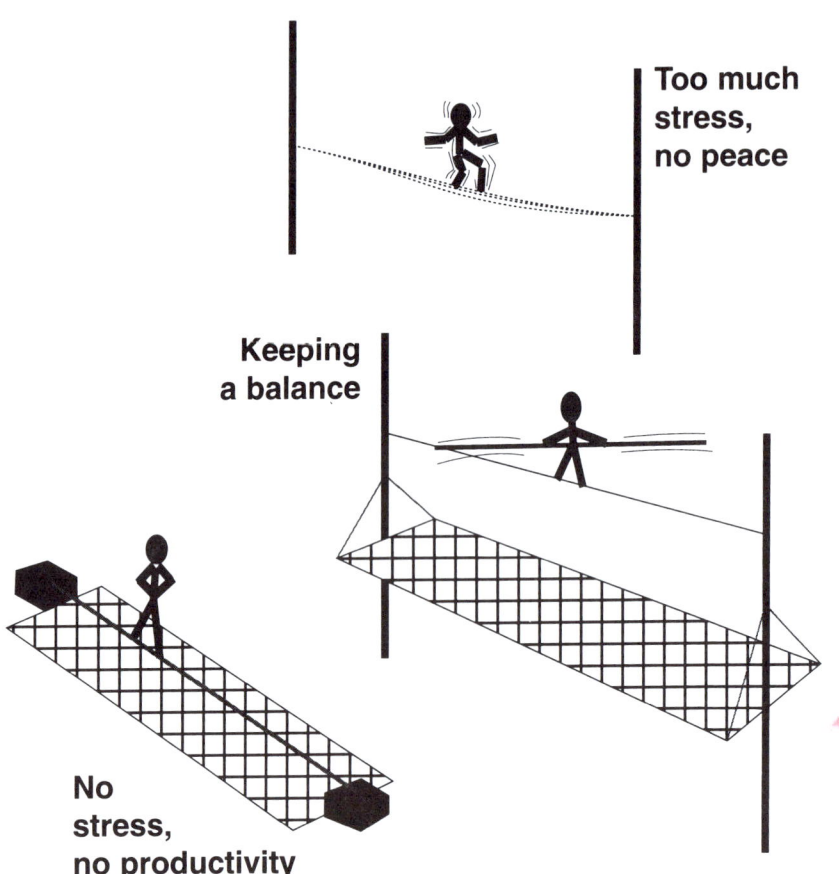

What Stress Is

How stress presents itself

One of the ways to know where we stand in relation to stress in our lives is to have a heightened awareness of how stress presents itself. Stress shows up through a series of signs and symptoms. A *sign* is a condition that is observable. A *symptom* is what a person actually experiences. The signs and symptoms vary from person to person. Stress doesn't affect everyone in exactly the same way. Let's look at some of the most common ways that stress presents itself. On the following pages is a Personal Stress Awareness Inventory. Review each of these items and check those that you have experienced in the last six months. Take inventory of your thoughts and feelings. Note if you've checked more items in one area than another. What does the inventory show you about your personal stress situation? A person's situation may be concentrated more in one area than another. However, stress affects the total person.

Personal Stress Awareness Inventory

Physical signs and symptoms

____ Increased susceptibility to illness
____ Lack of energy
____ Feeling weak
____ Insomnia (inability to sleep)
____ Frequent headaches
____ Muscle tightness
____ Change in eating habits (being very hungry or loss of appetite)
____ Change in weight
____ Chronic fatigue
____ Frequent colds
____ Nightmares
____ Nausea
____ Back or neck pain
____ Sleeping extended hours as a means of escape
____ Changes in bowel habits

Psychological/emotional signs and symptoms

_____ Depression
_____ Feeling of abandonment
_____ Desire to cry
_____ Forgetfulness
_____ Irritability
_____ Nervousness
_____ Fear
_____ Anxiety
_____ Negative self-concept
_____ Negative concept about your work
_____ Wanting to die
_____ Daydreaming as a means of escape
_____ Frequent absences from work
_____ Frequent arguments
_____ Inability to set limits
_____ Loss of interest in enjoyable activities
_____ Hopelessness
_____ Loss of concentration
_____ Confusion
_____ Preoccupation
_____ Sadness
_____ Loneliness
_____ Unrelinquished anger
_____ Thoughts about committing suicide
_____ Negative concept of life
_____ Frequent postponement of work
_____ Frequent late arrivals at work
_____ Overworking on a regular basis

Spiritual signs and symptoms

_____ Angry at yourself
_____ Angry at someone else
_____ Difficulty with worship and/or prayer
_____ Apathy towards church
_____ No longer reading the Bible
_____ Doubtful of personal salvation
_____ Feeling unworthy of forgiveness
_____ Angry at life in general
_____ Angry at God
_____ "God doesn't hear my prayers."
_____ Lack of attendance at church
_____ Feeling abandoned by God
_____ Doubtful of your calling
_____ Feeling abandoned by the church
_____ Feeling unworthy of God's love

There have been times when persons have checked most or all of the items on this list. Some were church leaders, ministers, and pastors. Others were seminary students or their spouses. No one is immune to stress. Neither should we feel embarrassed or ashamed if we feel that our stress is out of control. The important thing is to learn what stress is and how to use it for our benefit and not allow stress to be a destructive force in our lives.

Several years ago, I was leading a conference on stress for a group of pastors. A few wives also attended. After completing the exercise above, one of the pastors showed me that he had checked off the entire list of symptoms. He wanted help. My first response was to suggest that he talk to another pastor of the same cultural group. This pastor preferred to speak Spanish. He said, "We don't do that." Then I suggested that he talk to a pastor of the same faith, but a different cultural group. He responded, "We don't do that either." I asked if he would feel comfortable looking up a Christian counseling service in the telephone directory. There was silence. I caught myself wanting to problem-solve without knowing enough about the special needs of pastoral families. I decided to honor the silence.

We had been in group sessions for several days. During this time, I had noticed a sense of personal struggle in this pastor. His anguish was visible, although he was quiet and reserved. As we stood there facing each other in silence, he said, "There's a seminary where I live. I'll look for help there." And he did. Several weeks later, I learned that he was receiving professional counseling and was feeling better.

This was the first conference I had presented on stress. It was the first conference with a pastoral group. How little I knew about their special needs. As I reflected on this situation, I realized how difficult some church leaders, ministers, and pastors find it to confide about personal matters with each other. It's not easy to risk personal disclosure if you're supposed to be a spiritual leader. What will the other church leaders, ministers, and pastors think? What if my church members find out? Am I not right with God? Is this a sign of weakness? Is it a lack of faith? Satan takes advantage of our vulnerability during stressful times in our lives and capitalizes on burying our senses in doubt, embarrassment, and self-pity. These thoughts and feelings blind us from seeking positive solutions. We're too entangled and wrapped up in our pain. And that's exactly where Satan wants Christians to stay. Unchanged. Satan tries to convince us that we don't need to make any changes. We don't need to problem-solve. If we reach a state of mental, emotional, and spiritual paralysis, we become ineffective. Being in this condition limits our ability to glorify God and to contribute to the building of His Kingdom.

But God has another plan. "He renews our hopes and heals our bodies" (Psalm 147:3). ". . . You listened and pulled me from a lonely pit . . . you gave me a new song, a song of praise to you" (from Psalm 40:1-3).

Whether you are a church leader or a church member, be sensitive to notice signs of stress in the body of the church. I'm not suggesting that we go about the church with a microscopic eye to detect stress in each other. What I am saying is that we have a Christian responsibility to minister to each other in difficult times in our lives. Today I may reach out to help someone else. Tomorrow I may be the one who needs help. To be a healing agent for the body of Christ, we must be sensitive to need and willing to take steps to assist in the restoration of well-being.

Note that when Hezakiah was at the point of death, God said to him, "I heard you pray, and I saw you cry. I will heal you ..." (2 Kings 20:5*b*).

Two choices
Stress will affect us in one of two ways. It can help us, or it can hurt us. You and I have two choices. We can respond to stress *positively* and help ourselves. Or we can respond to stress *negatively* and hurt ourselves and sometimes others. The situation, problem, or factor causing the stress is *neutral*. You and I choose if we're going to gain any benefit from the situation or whether we'll become victims of stress. There are persons who go through life feeling victimized and helpless. They go through life believing that there's nothing they can do to pull themselves loose from the grip of unresolved negative stress. That's not so. Life doesn't have to be that way. We have some choices. In partnership with Christ, we *can* overcome. It really doesn't matter what type of problem we have or how difficult it may be. Stress can be harnessed in one direction or another: positive or negative, helpful or destructive. Which direction it goes is a personal choice.

2
The Importance of Perception

A university professor divided his class into two sections and asked one half of the class to close their eyes and the other half of the class to view Image A, which he projected on the screen as follows:

He told the viewing half of the class to take a hard look at the image projected and to remember what they had seen. Then he reversed the activity. He asked the first half of the class to close their eyes and showed Image B to the second half of the class. He also asked them to take a hard look at the image projected on the screen and to remember what they had seen.

The Importance of Perception 17

The professor then put Image C on the board and asked the two groups to look at the image and tell what they saw.

The students who had looked at Image A earlier saw Image A again, a beautiful, glamorous young woman. The students who had looked at Image B earlier saw Image B again, an unattractive old woman. Perception is a learned behavior. We tend to see that which we know.

How we view and how we respond to stress in our lives is also largely determined by what we have experienced and how we learned to respond to situations throughout our lives. Two people could be looking at the very same thing and see something different. Their perception will depend on how they were raised and how they choose to view things.

Human beings are creatures of habit. We grow up eating certain foods, dressing a certain way, speaking a certain way, and thinking a certain way. So it's understandable that we also tend to resist change.

The same thing happens with attitudes and feelings. Once these are formed, we want to hold on to them. It takes effort to change, and change may also be painful. When a person grows up in an environment lacking love and acceptance, that person is likely to perceive life differently than a person who grew up in an environment feeling loved and accepted. Love and acceptance is not part of the flavor of life for someone who has not experienced it. There's a void, a lingering loneliness, an emptiness in his or her life. Unresolved stress has a strong grip. "Worry is a heavy burden" (Proverbs 12:25*a*). Proverbs 17:22*b* says, "if you are sad, you hurt all over." Unless that oppressive chain is broken, some people go through life with the belief that that's the way life is supposed to be—negative and painful.

It's been said that some people die at 15 years of age but don't get buried until they're 52. Even dying at 52 years of age would be considered a premature death. They go throughout their lives without a sense of purpose or direction. Eventually, they fall victims to the ravages of negativity and unresolved stress.

A person who has experienced love and acceptance can overcome the grip of stress and turn any life circumstances into victorious living. For the Christian, this means seeking God's face. It means depending on Him, not on ourselves. It means seeking His truth in the Scriptures. Victorious living requires prayer and a total commitment to Jesus Christ. "If you know what you're doing, you will prosper. God blesses everyone who trusts him"

(Proverbs 16:20). This is the positive response to stress. Choosing the positive way doesn't mean it will be an easy way out of difficulty. Neither does it mean that things will turn out the way we would want them to. The assurance we have through Christ is that God gives us the grace to make it through. God said, "My kindness is all you need. My power is strongest when you are weak" (2 Corinthians 12:9).

Going back to our Christian roots, of all the role models in the Bible, Jesus Christ is the ideal example for us to learn how to manage stress successfully. My prayer is that you learn to perceive stress through the eyes of Jesus Christ, and that you incorporate biblical teachings as responses to stress in your daily life. The approaches that we will identify for dealing with stress successfully don't come from man's scientific discoveries. They're straight from the Bible, the living Word of God. "What God has said isn't only alive and active! It is sharper than any double-edged sword. His word can cut through our spirits and souls and through our joints and marrow, until it discovers the desires and thoughts of our hearts" (Hebrews 4:12). "Your word is a lamp that gives light wherever I walk" (Psalm 119:105).

Basic concepts about stress
- Stress is the body's response to a stimulus.
- The stimulus may be internal or external.
- Stress is a universal human experience.
- Stress is everywhere in our environment.
- We respond to stress mentally, emotionally, physically, and spiritually.
- We have two choices in dealing with stress. We can respond positively to stress and use that experience for our benefit. Or we can respond negatively and become victims of stress.
- The choice of how we respond to stress is our own.
- Jesus Christ is the ideal example for us to learn how to manage stress successfully.

Checking your personal level of stress

This "life-change units" stress questionnaire is based on the original work by Dr. Thomas H. Holmes and Dr. Richard H. Rahe (1967). It measures stressors experienced within a period of 12 months. Each stressor has a point value. Place a check mark by those events that have occurred in your life in the last 12 months. Total your score at the end of the questionnaire.

Death of spouse	_____	100
Divorce	_____	73
Marital separation	_____	65
Jail term	_____	63
Death of a close family member	_____	63
Personal injury or illness	_____	53
Marriage	_____	50
Fired at work	_____	47
Marital reconciliation	_____	45
Retirement	_____	45
Change in health of a family member	_____	44
Pregnancy	_____	40
Sexual difficulty	_____	40
Gaining a new family member	_____	39
Major business readjustment	_____	39
Major change in financial state	_____	38
Death of a close friend	_____	37
Change to a different line of work	_____	36
Increase in the number of arguments with spouse	_____	35
Taking on a mortgage	_____	31
Foreclosure on a mortgage or loan	_____	30
Change in responsibilities at work (promotion, demotion, transfer)	_____	29
Son or daughter leaving home	_____	29
Trouble with in-laws	_____	29
Outstanding personal achievement	_____	28
Spouse beginning or stopping work outside the home	_____	26
Going back to school	_____	26

Change in living conditions
    (building a new home, remodeling,
    deterioration of home) _____ 25
Revision of personal habits _____ 24
Trouble with boss _____ 23
Change in work hours or conditions _____ 20
Change in residence _____ 20
Change to a new school _____ 20
Change in type and/or amount of
    recreation _____ 19
Change in church activities _____ 19
Change in social activities _____ 18
Purchasing a car, or other big purchases _____ 17
Change in sleeping habits _____ 16
Change in number of family get-togethers _____ 15
Change in eating habits _____ 15
Vacation _____ 13
Christmas or holiday observances _____ 12
Minor violations of the law (traffic tickets) _____ 11

                      Total   _____

Multiply the value by the number of times the event occurred. Then total all your scores. If your total is between 150 and 300, you have a 51 percent chance of developing an illness or disease within two years. If the score is 300 points or above, there is a high risk or an 80 percent chance of developing an illness or a disease in the following two years.[6] Examine the result of your score carefully. If your score is over 300 points, take a close look at what is going on in your life. It may be necessary to make some changes.

3
Responses to Stress

Psychological/emotional responses
Earlier we outlined some of the common signs and symptoms of stress. In the psychological/emotional area, stress can show through withdrawal. Some people choose to isolate themselves from others. They may go to the extreme of locking themselves in a room, shutting the blinds, and refusing to eat or see or talk to anyone. Others demonstrate their stress through irritability. The family complains about the person's bad moods and aggressive behavior. They make those around them feel uncomfortable not knowing when the angry person will strike at someone. The bad moods and aggressive behavior are sometimes seen at the workplace. The frustrations are not kept at home.

Nervousness, fearfulness, or anxiety are other responses to stress. While we may experience these feelings during a stressful situation, once the situation is resolved these feelings should not linger. These feelings indicate a disequilibrium in a person's life if they continue beyond the resolution of the problem.

Some of the responses to stress show at the opposite ends of a continuum. For example, there are those persons who respond to stress by overworking. They are so involved in their work that they become oblivious to the world around them. They may even feel good about being so busy. In some cases, people attach a sense of self-worth to their work. The harder they work, the more valuable they believe they are. Pastors have shared that they perceived themselves as being faithful to their calling to the degree that they were tired at the end of the day. In other words, the more tired they felt, the more faithful they were. This perception existed until they found themselves staring at the ceiling of a hospital room while recovering from a heart attack.

On the other hand, there are others who respond to stress by avoiding work. They start arriving late at their place of employment until tardiness becomes a pattern. Then they progress to missing work. Neither their head nor their heart is in their work. Life circumstances can get so demanding and complicated that a person may feel like giving up. They question whether life is worth living. This brings thoughts of suicide, wanting to die. A red flag should go up in our minds if this happens. It can be a fleeing thought while one is under extreme pressure. It is a very dangerous sign if the thought of ending one's life lingers. It is best to seek professional help in this case.

Another sign of psychological and emotional stress is holding on to anger. Imagine that each one of us carries an invisible bag on his shoulder. As we encounter disappointments, barriers, arguments, annoyances, and other negative obstacles during the day, we throw them into our invisible bag. This bag needs to be emptied by the end of each day, preferably through humble prayer. What often happens, though, is that we pile one negative experience upon another, failing to empty the bag, until the weight becomes so heavy that we become entangled with the negative impact of unresolved anger. In some cases, this anger may go back for years. It has developed deep roots over time. A person may live for years with the attitude, "I'll get even one of these days," all to his or her personal detriment. Because of holding on to anger, they (not the source of the anger) end up with an ulcerated stomach or a heart attack.

Physical signs and symptoms
Physical signs and symptoms of stress also present themselves at opposite ends of the continuum. For example, some people respond to stress by overeating. Others stop eating. Either extreme is dangerous. An overweight woman goes shopping for a dress and can't find one that fits. She blames the store. She feels depressed and goes home and eats a whole pie, instead of a slice. She feels better afterwards. Then she goes back to shop for a dress. When she can't find a nice-looking dress that she can fit into, she becomes depressed again, and the cycle repeats itself. This is a behavioral pattern of unresolved stress.

While some persons develop diarrhea as a response to stress, others become constipated. Some people complain of being unable to sleep. Others can't wake up. Some people become more susceptible to illness. Some experience frequent colds. Others may complain of always feeling tired. They go to bed tired, and they wake up tired. Frequent headaches, muscle tightness, and back or neck pain are common symptoms of stress. Some skin irritations may also erupt as a result of stress. Our body talks to us and tells us that we need help. It is to our benefit to be sensitive to the signs and symptoms of stress.

Spiritual signs and symptoms
The spiritual side of stress is the area we tend to hide or ignore the most. One reason for this is the misconception that life for Christians should be so well ordered that they should not have stress. In other words, if a Christian is experiencing stress, then something must be wrong in his or her life, with his or her relationship with God. So Christians who are having difficulties in life are shamed into hiding them. They don't want to be labeled as weak or failures, so denial becomes an avoidance behavior. The smile on the face hides the hemorrhaging in the heart.

Spiritual signs and symptoms of stress are characterized by anger, also. There may be anger at oneself, anger at someone else, anger at life in general, or anger at God. This anger translates into anger at the church. There may be a spirit of condemnation towards the church-going Christian. The perceived relationship becomes one of "them, the hypocrites" and "me." Criticism may be launched beginning with the pastor, then his wife and children, then the deacons, followed by the music director, and the list goes on and on.

The negativity may progress to being doubtful of one's personal salvation, doubtful of one's calling, feeling unworthy of forgiveness, and feeling abandoned by God. There may be doubt that God hears his prayers, so he quits reading the Bible. Praying becomes distant, and apathy sets in. This may be the person you'll see sitting at the very back of the church when he does attend. There is no interest in taking part in anything. He may have the ability to teach, but he doesn't want to do so. He doesn't want to sing. He doesn't want to help in any way.

The paradox is that after a while we leave him alone with the "who wants him anyway?" mentality. Yet, it may be exactly during this time of negativity that he most needs someone to reach out to him. This may be the only way he knows to ask for help. We must look behind and beyond the obvious, the signs of unresolved stress, and share a word of encouragement, extend a handshake, show love and acceptance. Our sensitivity must precede any judgmental conclusion about the person's condition.

Take a look at your medicine cabinet
When we are experiencing stress in unhealthy proportions, our body will talk to us by using some of the signals we have just mentioned, although everyone experiences stress differently. A barometer to gauge how we are listening to our bodies is the medicine cabinet. Take a look at your medicine cabinet. Do you have a lineup of antacids? Do you pop antacid pills all day long to control your nervous stomach? When you go to the drug section of the supermarket, do you look for the bottles that are labeled *extra strength* when you are filling up on medication for aches and pains, for improved sleep, for bowel control, for fast weight loss, for stamina?

Sometimes we convince ourselves that we're too busy to see a doctor if any of the signs and symptoms of stress persist. We'll try to appease the discomfort by self-prescription. If you do go to see a doctor and complain of not being able to sleep well, you may get a prescription for medication to help you sleep better. If your complaint is that you can't seem to wake up, you may get a prescription to help you be more alert. If you have high blood pressure, you'll get medication to help you control your high blood pressure. If you have diabetes, you'll get medication to help control the diabetes. If you have depression, you may get a prescription for an antidepressant. The question that you may not get asked is, "What is going on in your life?" If you are ignoring this question, and the physician is not raising this question, you are setting yourself up for *payday*. Payday is the day when your body (psychological, emotional, physical, and spiritual) is going to tell you, "I have been giving you signs and symptoms. I have given you many warnings, but you chose to ignore them. Now you must pay. I can't sustain life any more under these circumstances. Make some changes or die."

Our body is like a mattress spring. When it's new, pressure can be placed on it, and it will bounce back in place whenever the pressure is removed. If the mattress, however, has the weight of pressure on it over the years, it wears out. When pressure is applied, it no longer bounces back into place after the pressure is relieved. It stays compressed and out of shape. Our bodies do the same thing. When we subject ourselves to the pressures of daily living without some constructive relief, over time, our body is depleted of its ability to *bounce back* into shape. It cripples under sustained unresolved stress. When this condition persists without change, the body ultimately collapses and dies.

If you stop and think about it, you probably know of someone who died prematurely due to unresolved stress. Don't let it happen to you. Try to keep it from happening to someone you love. Knowledge is power. Ignorance is dangerous. The truth is freedom. (See John 8:31-32.)

We have looked at the definition of stress and have identified some of the sources of stress. We have also reviewed indicators of stress in three categories: psychological/emotional, physical, and spiritual, and we have identified some of the responses to stressors in these areas. The question now is, *How do we deal with stress?* In the following chapters, we are going to look at spiritual keys to manage stress successfully. The first key is to take inventory of sources of stress in your life today. The second key is to listen to your body. Hear what your body is telling you. The third key is to maintain a balance in life. We'll start with the first key.

4
Keys for Managing Stress

There are three keys for managing stress. The first one is to take inventory of the stress factors in our lives. The second key is to listen to our bodies by paying attention to the stages of alarm, resistance, and exhaustion. The third key to managing stress in our lives is to maintain a healthy and balanced lifestyle. Let's look at each of these keys individually. As you read, take time to answer the questions, apply the statements to your life, and determine ways to better manage stress and live a more peaceful and balanced life.

Key 1: Take inventory of stress factors in your life today

Think about yourself. Is there something about yourself that is bothering you? When you look at yourself in the mirror every morning, do you see someone you like? Do you see someone you respect? Do you see someone you love? How do you feel about yourself? I'm not referring to whether you like the shape of your nose or the color of your eyes. I'm talking about your inner self. Are you at peace with yourself?

What about your family? Are you experiencing any difficulties with your family? If you are single, how is your relationship with your family? If you are married, how is your relationship with your spouse, your children, the extended family? Some of the most common sources of stress are ineffective communication in the family and financial matters. Most of the stress in families involves either one or both of these issues. Husbands identify poor communication with the wife, and the wife identifies poor communication with the husband. Both parents tend to identify problems in communication with their children. Young people tend to identify poor communication with their parents as a major source of stress.

St. Clair writes:
"With well over half the teenagers living in single parent homes, and over 65 percent of all mothers working outside the home, it is little wonder that parents don't spend time with their kids. According to George Barna, among teens whose father is present in the home, the average amount of time discussing things that matter is less than 40 minutes per week. ... In homes where the mother is present, the amount of time spent with her discussing matters of interest to the teen averages 55 minutes per week.[7]

Let's pause to take a more in-depth look at some of the dynamics of the contemporary family. Whether the mother works outside the home or not, chances are she has had a full day of work by the time dinner needs to be prepared. Does she turn to her husband and say, "Honey, it's your turn to get dinner ready"? In most cases, the answer is no. She cooks, serves, and cleans afterwards. There's the table to clear. Dishes need to be washed, dried, and placed in the cupboard. There are floors to sweep and mop, and clothes to wash, dry, fold, and put up. Less often, there may be clothes to iron. That's not all. There also needs to be milk in the refrigerator, cereal for breakfast, gas in the car. Little Johnny's clothes need to be sorted so that they match when he goes to school in the morning. There are bills to pay. Kids need help with homework, and the school needs homemade cookies for the class party.

It's 11:30 p.m. The mother feels that she can barely make it into bed. Her husband is already asleep snoring. He faces the wall. He too is tired. He works two jobs to make ends meet. When the kids needed help with the homework, the father sent them to the mother. The mother sent them to him. Neither one of them helped. So their child goes to school and sits in the back of the classroom embarrassed because he didn't do his homework. Mom and Dad were too busy and tired, *for the right reasons*— keeping bread on the table, surviving the demands of daily living.

Families with children have additional stressors. A principle one is child care for the younger children and/or after-school care for the older children. The younger children are dropped off at a day care center for the largest part of the child's waking hours.

The older children come home after school, if they do go home, to an empty house. The television set becomes the caregiver. It's mechanical, full of violence, and strong in impact.

Parents continue to work long hours *for the right reasons*. No one is going to argue with parents who work to provide for their families. Most of the time we find justification for being stressed, over-extended, even burned-out. By the time students graduate from high school, they will have watched 15,000 hours of television, which translates to 3,000 hours in excess of the time spent in the classroom.[8] The American Academy of Pediatrics emphasizes the need to curtail television viewing to "not more than two hours a day in order to limit the damage caused by violence and sexual programming."[9] The problem is the absentee parent.

The teens in the family want nice clothes. They don't want cheap blue jeans and tennis shoes. These need to have designer names, just like the ones the other kids have. If they need transportation to go to school or work, they don't want an old car. It needs to be a nice car, just like the other kids. Peer pressure. Drugs and alcohol. Sex. All are competing for the youth's attention. Then parents wonder why they can't communicate with their children anymore. A consequence of this family lifestyle is that what should be a home becomes an aggregate of people sharing physical space but lacking mental, emotional, and spiritual unity.

So the wife finally makes it to bed feeling tired and overextended. She crawls into bed and falls asleep facing the opposite wall. This scenario happens in many families from time to time. Problems arise when it becomes a way of life. It can happen so often in some households that after a while, it becomes a pattern, an effortless routine. Chronic overextension becomes the norm for the parents, and the children learn to cope in their absence. Or do they? Families can work themselves into a pattern of dysfunction. Dysfunction is habit-forming. As time goes on, the family is no longer a cohesive unit.

As chronic overextension sets in with the parents, so does separation. The separation may start physically. Then it becomes emotional and mental, and progresses to a spiritual distance. The husband begins to sleep in the boys' room or the couch. After a while, he may quit coming home. Some wives do the same thing. Eventually, they too quit coming home. There are no pillars left for a household to stand on, much less a home or a family.

The irony of it all is that the couple set out to work long hours *for the right reasons.* Satan manages to trick Christians into believing that they were doing the right thing. He wants the parents tired and worn out because they become more vulnerable to his attacks. The mental, physical, and spiritual resistance is low. The whole family suffers.

One day, the couple wakes up. They're retired. They're no longer rushing anywhere. The jobs they once had are now being carried out by somebody else. Somebody else is preaching, making home visits, visiting hospital patients, visiting prisoners, counseling, and dealing with the deacon body. Somebody else is leading the missions work of the church, managing the nursery, planning banquets, playing the piano, and directing the Christmas play. Somebody else is the executive director. Somebody else has taken over the classroom. Somebody else has taken their place. And all this time they thought they were indispensable!

They're having coffee at their kitchen table and find themselves staring at each other. The kids are gone, each with his or her own family. The husband and wife look at each other and realize that they really don't know each other. They've slept in the same bed, shopped at the same stores, had a joint bank account. They've gone to the same church. They've sat in the same pew, attended the same Sunday School, sang in the same choir. Yet, they *really* don't know each other. Even worse, they don't *love* each other. It's a stark revelation! All those years of being together have been years of mutual convenience. There was food. A change of clothes. A place to sleep. But not much more. Then they wonder why the kids don't call home. The kids may never tell the parents directly, but they feel that mom and dad didn't have time for them when they were growing up, so why should they bother with them now? Parental abandonment is a common complaint among children of church leaders, ministers, and pastors. Family abandonment is a common complaint among pastoral wives. Unresolved stress is the pathway of opportunity that Satan uses to cause conflict and separation in Christian families.

So it's not unusual these days to hear of couples in their senior years parting ways. Other Christian couples aren't waiting. They are divorcing or separating in growing numbers. In some cultures, divorce is not acceptable. When divorce is not a socially acceptable option, couples live apart. Separation may be more tolerable from a sociocultural perspective. The pain and disappointment of a failed marriage and a divided family is no less hurtful.

With the growing emphasis on the acquisition of material things as a measure of achievement and success, the Christian family must remain alert to the insidiousness of stress as the devil's tactic to get the family sidetracked. After all, it takes one individual in the family and only one incident to derail a whole family. One family can derail a whole church. Satan knows that if he can derail families and churches, he can ultimately take over whole communities. And he wouldn't want to stop there. His ambition is to conquer the world. We must fight for the preservation of the Christian family. Healthy individuals make healthy families. Healthy families make healthy churches. Healthy churches can make a positive difference for Christ in the community.

Where do you stand with stress in your life today? If stress affects you so much that it has also affected your family, it's time to face the problem and find healthy solutions.

Five questions
The following questions can help you take an inventory of factors that are causing stress in your life today. Take time to think through these questions and answer them as directly as possible. Sometimes it may be difficult to face your need. This is a starting place for healing and restoration of mind, body, and spirit. You may want to write down your answers.

- In your life today, what factors are causing stress?
- In what way(s) is this stress affecting you?
- What action(s) have you taken?
- What results have you had?
- Is it necessary for you to make some changes? What changes?

I mentioned earlier that Jesus Christ is the best role model for dealing with stress. Let's take a look at some biblical examples and take special note of the actions used to counteract the negative effects of stress.

Spiritual markers for taking inventory of stress

Biblical direction
- "Then he went up on a mountain where he could be alone and pray. Later that evening, he was still there" (Matthew 14:23).

- "Then Jesus said, 'Let's go to a place where we can be alone and get some rest.'" (Mark 6:31*b*).

- "If you are tired from carrying heavy burdens, come to me and I will give you rest. Take the yoke I give you. Put it on your shoulders and learn from me. I am gentle and humble, and you will find rest. This yoke is easy to bear, and this burden is light" (Matthew 11:28-30).

Action
- Be alone to pray.

- Retrieve to a quiet place to rest.

- Accept the invitation from Christ to give Him your burdens.

- Christ gives the promise, "I will give you rest."

- Christ calls our attention to the nature of his heart: "I am gentle and humble . . .".

- Christ calls us to be in a dual yoke with Him and to "learn" from Him. He promises again, "you will find rest." With Christ, the yoke is easy and the load is light.

Many cultural groups value personal independence and self-reliance. In the U.S., we are socialized from an early age to do for ourselves. This idea becomes so much a part of our thinking that, even as Christians, we find it difficult to let go and let Christ take charge. How many times have we gone to the altar to pray on our knees, asking God to help us in our time of need, only to get up off of our knees still carrying the load we supposedly prayed to have lifted?

Sometimes our attitudes and behaviors show distrust of God's infinite wisdom and power. We act as if God needs our help to bring relief to our lives. He clearly wants us to turn to Him: "If you are tired from carrying heavy burdens, come to me..." (Matthew 11:28). We need to approach God in prayer with the positive expectancy that He will respond. God is faithful. His response may be *yes*, *no*, or *wait*, but He will respond. The psalmist wrote in Psalm 46: "God is our mighty fortress, always ready to help in times of trouble.... The LORD All-Powerful is with us. The God of Jacob is our fortress" (vv.1, 11). "When I am in trouble, I pray, knowing you will listen" (Psalm 86:7).

I can attest to the difficulty of "letting go." There have been times when I felt as if I were driving in thick fog. Even having the headlights on did not help, because I still could not see much further ahead of me. I've had a sense of helplessness and exasperation overcome me.

One of those times was in 1983. In January of that year, my sister was admitted to the hospital with a heart condition. A few days after she was released, my younger brother was diagnosed with leukemia. He was admitted to a major medical center for treatment. A few months later, my father was admitted to the same medical center for a growth in one of his lungs. He underwent surgery and developed serious complications. Two loved ones were dying at the same time, one at one location of the medical center and the other at another.

As a registered nurse, I understood what the prognosis was. Not good. I had just begun my recovery from my mother's death. The grief was unbearable. There were times when I wondered if God even cared about my family or me. As the months wore on, there were times when I prayed to die. I didn't want to live any longer. I had reached the end of my rope. But God was merciful. In my silent screams from the innermost depth of my being, He comforted me with "If you are tired from carrying heavy burdens, come to me and I will give you rest" (Matthew 11:28).

Dad died in July. He never left the hospital for the last four months of his life. Richard died a few weeks later shortly after his thirty-ninth birthday. He had been hospitalized for nine months. Almost fifteen years have gone by since that time. I rest in the knowledge that Mom, Dad, and Richard were believers.

The Lord has also restored my peace. "Pray that our LORD will make us strong and give us peace" (Psalm 29:11).

In 1 Peter 5:6-7 we find another quality of human character designed to help us manage stress. It is part of the discipline required of us to let go of our burden and to allow God to transform the situation into an opportunity for us to know Him better. The verses read, "Be humble in the presence of God's mighty power, and he will honor you when the time comes. God cares for you, so turn all your worries over to him." Humility frees our minds and our hearts to make room for the Holy Spirit to do His work. Humility is a prerequisite for transformation, healing, and restoration from within. The believer will be exalted "when the time comes." The apostle reminds us to give *all*—not just some—of our worries to Him. In 2 Corinthians 3:17, Paul writes, "The Lord and the Spirit are one and the same, and the Lord's Spirit sets us free."

The biblical approach to managing stress does not make Christians immune from the stressors of daily living. It does provide, however, a Christ-centered perspective for responding to stressors. If your stress level is so high that you feel helpless and out of control, read Psalm 23. It's a source of comfort in trying times.

"You, LORD, are my shepherd.
   I will never be in need.
You let me rest in fields
   of green grass.
You lead me to streams
of peaceful water,
   and you refresh my life.

You are true to your name,
and you lead me
   along the right paths.
I may walk through valleys
as dark as death,
   but I won't be afraid.

You are with me,
and your shepherd's rod
   makes me feel safe.
You treat me to a feast,
   while my enemies watch.
You honor me as your guest,
and you fill my cup]
   until it overflows.
Your kindness and live
will always be with me
   each day of my life,
and I will live forever
   in your house, LORD."
               —*Psalm 23*

Psalm 139 speaks about God's presence everywhere and His complete knowledge of us. Particularly in very difficult times when we might be so overwhelmed with our life circumstances that we feel abandoned, forgotten, or insignificant, this Psalm reassures the Christian that God not only has a permeating, all-encompassing presence and knows everything, but He also cares. Psalm 139 is a beacon for navigating through the storm with a Christ-centered compass. "Or suppose I said, 'I'll hide in the dark until night comes to cover me over.' But you see in the dark because daylight and dark are all the same to you" (vv.11-12).

In this Psalm we also see the importance of being predisposed to allow God to work in our lives in order to align ourselves with His will. "Look deep into my heart, God, and find out everything I am thinking. Don't let me follow evil ways, but lead me in the way that time has proven true" (vv. 23-24).

Through a search of God's Word, we have identified several actions to counteract the negative impact of stress in our lives. These are:

• **Take time to be alone.** Ecclesiastes 3 affirms that there is a time for listening (v. 7). Quietness soothes the mind and the spirit. We can be alone without being lonely. Plan to spend time alone every day, even if it's just a few minutes. Focus on God in silence. Listen to what God has to say to you. "Our God says, 'Calm down, and learn that I am God! . . .' " (Psalm 46:10*a*).

• **Pray.** ". . . never stop praying" (1 Thessalonians 5:17). God already knows our need before we ever voice it. Praying raises *our* awareness of God's faithfulness. It brings our spirit in alignment with His Spirit. Prayer is the spiritual exercise for total wellness. It enables us to know God more and more, to fellowship with Him, and to love Him. Prayer is the umbilical cord that nurtures our total being now and even on to everlasting life. How wonderful it is to pray. What a privilege to have!

"I will answer their prayers before they finish praying" (Isaiah 65:24).
"Do what the LORD wants, and he will give you your heart's desire" (Psalm 37:4).
"So whenever we are in need, we should come bravely before the throne of our merciful God.

There we will be treated with undeserved kindness, and we will find help" (Hebrews 4:16).

• **Retreat to a quiet place.** This allows you the opportunity to decompress and re-group your thinking and re-charge your level of energy: mentally, emotionally, physically, and spiritually. Safeguard your peace. "Pray that our LORD will make us strong and give us peace" (Psalm 29:11).

• **Rest.** "Then he lay down in the shade and fell asleep" (1 Kings 19:5*a*). Several brief rest periods during the day may work well for you. Mental images of peaceful beauty can be stress relievers. Practice taking three or four deep breaths and picture stress leaving your body.

• **Turn over your burdens to Christ.** Think of your burden as a gift for Christ. Wrap it in your favorite wrapping paper. Choose your favorite color. Put ribbon and a bow on it. Picture yourself placing that gift at the foot of the cross. Leave it there. "You will worship me with all your heart, and I will be with you" (Jeremiah 29:13).

• **Assume a dual yoke with Christ.** "Christ gives me the strength to face anything" (Philippians 4:13). Arturo, my youngest brother, is nicknamed "Square." He's a big man. I greatly love and admire him. He became a millionaire in his thirties and later lost his fortune. Through it all, he has maintained a positive attitude. He shared with me recently, "Whatever problems I face each day, I know that God has already been there before me. This is my Christian belief." The Lord has prospered his family anew. "The Lord will lead you into the land. He will always be with you and help you, so don't ever be afraid of your enemies" (Deuteronomy 31:8). "But I will bless those who trust me. They will be like trees growing beside a stream—trees with roots that reach down to the water, and with leaves that are always green. They bear fruit every year and are never worried by a lack of rain" (Jeremiah 17:7-8).

• **Humble yourself before God.** "The way to please you is to feel sorrow deep in our hearts. This is the kind of sacrifice you won't refuse" (Psalm 51:17). Pray specifically for humility. Develop an attitude of humility. Practice humility. "Don't be jealous or proud, but be humble and consider others more important than yourselves" (Philippians 2:3). "The LORD . . . is kind to everyone who is humble" (Proverbs 3:34*b*).

• **Claim the promise.** "You, LORD, are my shepherd. I will never be in need" (Psalm 23:1). Learn to lean on God. He will show you the way. He may speak to you through a person, a letter, a telephone call, a book, a song. Sometimes He may speak in the way or time you least expected. "Our Lord and our God, you are like the sun and also like a shield. You treat us with kindness and with honor, never denying any good thing to those who live right" (Psalm 84:11). "But without faith no one can please God. We must believe that God is real and that he rewards everyone who searches for him" (Hebrews 11:6).

• **Believe that God cares for you and your situation.** "I promise to take care of them and keep them safe . . ." (Ezekiel 34:15). "Would any of you give your hungry child a stone, if the child asked for some bread? Would you give your child a snake if the child asked for a fish? As bad as you are, you still know how to give good gifts to your children. But your heavenly Father is even more ready to give good things to people who ask" (Matthew 7:9-11).

• **Be willing to make changes.** "Anyone who belongs to Christ is a new person. The past is forgotten, and everything is new" (2 Corinthians 5:17). "I have died, but Christ lives in me. And I now live by faith in the Son of God, who loved me and gave his life for me" (Galatians 2:20). Making changes does not come naturally or easily to most people. Refusal to change is the holding cell that Satan uses to deny us freedom in Christ. But change is possible through Christ. ". . . I forget what is behind, and I struggle for what is ahead. I run toward the goal, so that I can win the prize of being called to heaven. This is the prize that God offers because of what Christ Jesus has done" (Philippians 3:13-14).

• **Make room for the Holy Spirit to transform your life.** "If you love me, you will do as I command. Then I will ask the

Father to send you the Holy Spirit who will help you and always be with you" (John 14:15-16). "God's kingdom isn't about eating and drinking. It is about pleasing God, about living in peace, and about true happiness. All this comes from the Holy Spirit" (Romans 14:17)."I pray that God, who gives hope, will bless you with complete happiness and peace because of your faith. And may the power of the Holy Spirit fill you with hope" (Romans 15:13).

• **Give thanks to God for His faithfulness.** "[You] treated me so kindly that I don't need to worry anymore" (Psalm 116:7). "God can be trusted, and he chose you to be partners with his Son, our Lord Jesus Christ" (1 Corinthians 1:9). "We should be grateful that we were given a kingdom that cannot be shaken. And in this kingdom we please God by worshiping him and by showing him great honor and respect" (Hebrews 12:28). "Our sacrifice is to keep offering praise to God in the name of Jesus" (Hebrews 13:15).

As Christians, we will find ourselves engaged in spiritual warfare on a daily basis. Satan works nonstop to attack the Christian's self-esteem and sense of self-worth. He aims to attack the mind and achieve spiritual paralysis. He tries to convince the believer that his or her sin is greater than God's willingness to forgive. Satan wants the Christian entangled in a web of guilt, self-contempt, and hopelessness. Uncontrolled stress serves to separate us from communion with God. It can numb our desire to fellowship with Him. It trips us into a hole of self-pity, a state of discouragement. Uncontrolled stress has a blinding effect. It shuts out the light and the truth from our lives. This is contrary to God's will.

". . . the LORD will save you from all of your sins" (Psalm 130:8).
"With all my heart, I am waiting, LORD, for you! I trust your promises" (Psalm 130:5).
". . . our God, you are merciful and quick to forgive; you are loving, kind, and very patient" (Nehemiah 9:17*a*).

The spiritual gateway to control stress is not a matter of the mind. It begins with a spiritual desire to know God. "Show me your paths and teach me to follow; guide me by your truth and instruct me. You keep me safe, and I always trust you" (Psalm 25:4-5). Successful stress management then becomes a series of learned behaviors, a way of life. "I have shown you the way that makes sense; I have guided you along the right path" (Proverbs 4:11). "You said to me, 'I will point out the road that you should follow. I will be your teacher and watch over you'" (Psalm 32:8). As Christians, we do not accept defeat from the destructive forces of uncontrolled stress. Satan loses. God wins.

Key 2: Listen to your body

A healthy person is someone who maintains a balance in his or her life mentally, emotionally, physically, and spiritually. A person can therefore be healthy even in the presence of disease or infirmity. Our body talks to us through signs and symptoms. These signs and symptoms can measure or indicate the level of stress in our lives. Hans Selye, the father of stress research, defined three types of responses to stress, noting them as a three-stage process.[10] These stages are known as the general adaptation syndrome.

Stage one: The alarm stage

In this stage, the body reacts with the *fight-or-flight response*. When faced with a threat in our environment, we must decide whether we will stand firm and fight or run away. The threat may be a surprising telephone call at 3:00 a.m., an argument, a close brush with what could have been a serious automobile accident, or anything that causes a change in our state of balance and triggers an adaptive response. Having positive experiences can also produce stress. Anticipation of a marriage, getting a promotion, or buying a house can also get a person off balance and cause stress. Whatever the cause, stress affects the body in the same way.

In this alarm stage, the body produces more adrenaline. The adrenaline bathes the body, causing a series of changes. Some of the most common physical changes when a person feels threatened are increased heart rate, rapid pulse, rapid breathing, dilatation of the pupils, and increased perspiration. All of our senses are heightened. We see better, hear better, and smell more acutely. There's increased muscle strength. Our gastric activity slows down. There's a decrease in the blood flow to the abdomen and body surface. These are all survival responses. Our body is designed to respond to the stressors in daily living. If the stressful experience is short-lived and put behind us, our body returns to a state of equilibrium or low arousal. However, if the stressful situation continues over an extended period of time, even months or years, the body enters the *stage of resistance*.

Stage two: The resistance stage
In the resistance stage, the body struggles to regain a state of balance but has difficulty in the face of unresolved stress. The body continues to produce adrenaline. This may even give us a false feeling of wellness. In this stage, stress develops roots which can ultimately lead to disease, disability, and death. What happens is that the body becomes accustomed to the maladjustment. The maladjustment becomes the norm. The longer we live with the problem, the more it becomes a part of our life. Stress works this way. We settle in with the discomfort or the pain in our lives. Sometimes we adopt the attitude that there is nothing we can do about the problem and choose to incorporate the stressor as a normal part of our life. When this occurs, we have given unresolved stress full freedom to cause damage to our health: physically, mentally, emotionally, and spiritually. Unresolved stress has a crippling effect. It doesn't explode suddenly. It builds over time only to show up later and claim a price on our well-being.

Our body continues to talk to us. It gives us headaches. We take headache medicine. It gives us muscle tension. We take medicine to relieve muscle tension. If we can't sleep, we take medicines to help us sleep. If we can't stay awake, we take medicines to give us energy. If we develop diabetes, the doctor prescribes medication to treat diabetes. If we develop high blood pressure, the doctor prescribes medication to treat the high blood pressure. But the root of the problem remains unchanged. In the case of overextended periods of unresolved stress, cardiovascular disease sets in. Dr. Archibald D. Hart notes, "The heart is the central target of destruction for much of the harmful stress we experience."[11]

A common message the body gives about unresolved stress is a body rash. A person with this problem may start out trying to treat the problem through a self-prescribed, over-the-counter medication, only to have the skin rash persist. Next he seeks medical help and starts taking cortisone, only to find that the rash still persists. Neither the over-the-counter medication or the cortisone can reach the mind and spirit where the healing needs to take place. Individuals have shared their experience of an unrelenting skin rash that appeared at the time they were dealing with a difficult issue in their lives. Medical treatment was to no avail. It wasn't until they dealt with the root of the problem, the issue causing them stress, that the body rash also went away.

Our bodies may also send a message through stomach pain. An initial response may be to ignore it. We try to go about our business as usual. Sometimes we blame the food or the condiments in the food. We blame the garlic, the hot sauce, or something else. This is usually followed by antacid medications, but to no avail. Antacids don't reach the root of the problem. The discomfort persists over time. When medical attention is finally sought, the pain is diagnosed as a bleeding ulcer, and the bleeding ulcer requires surgical intervention. This is one example of the high cost of unresolved stress.

Another frequent excuse for ignoring messages about stress overload is that we are too busy. In our minds, this is a good reason. We're too busy working. Sometimes we know what we are busy about. Other times we are so busy being busy that we forget what it is that we're supposed to be busy about. But, for the most part, we value work or the benefits that follow work. Therefore, we rationalize that being overworked is okay. In fact, in the stage of resistance, if we don't feel overextended and overworked, we may even feel that something is wrong. Something is missing in our lives. We have become so accustomed to the stress that it's like an addiction. In the meantime, not only are we overworking, but also we're trying to make sense of the rapid changes taking place around us. Our body systems are in an automatic accelerated pace, with the mental, emotional, physical, and spiritual shock absorbers wearing thin. The workaholic superman and superwoman of the late twentieth century fit this description.

Resistance to stress can also manifest itself in destructive action. Long-term stress can create a distance (physical, mental, emotional, and spiritual) between family, friends, classmates, and/or coworkers. It can sever communications and end relationships. It can lead to social isolation, introversion, and low self-esteem. These conditions are fertile grounds to harbor anger and hate, which in themselves are harmful. The mental and emotional pain may be so overwhelming that it leads to rages and killing sprees, many times causing the lives of innocent victims. In other situations, unresolved stress leads down the path of self-destruction, including suicide.

Unresolved stress claims victims of all ages. It doesn't have boundaries of gender, culture, position in life, religion, or country of origin. No one is immune to the devastation of unresolved stress.

Help is possible.
The critical question with healing potential that often is not asked is, *"What is going on in your life, and what are you doing about it?"* Paying attention to this question and answer can serve as a springboard to restoration, the way out of the stage of resistance. Help is still possible! There is hope. First, we must accept the fact that we have a problem. Second, we must want to get help. Third, we must seek help. Then we must work the plan.

Stage three: The exhaustion stage
In this stage the body systems shut down due to the chronic wear-and-tear of unresolved stress. If a person survives a heart attack at the stage of resistance but does not make any lifestyle changes, that person may not survive a second heart attack in the stage of exhaustion. The body's final message is, "I've talked to you over a long period of time. I've given you warnings, but they've gone unheeded. I can't continue to function anymore." And the person dies. The final message is death.

Listening to your body
We've looked at some of the dimensions of the three stages of stress: *the alarm stage, the resistance stage,* and *the exhaustion stage.* Now take time to listen and hear what your body has to tell you. Allow your body to tell you everything it wants you to hear: mentally, emotionally, physically, and spiritually. Jot down your thoughts as these come to mind. Don't try to sort through the

meaning of everything that you're thinking or feeling. Go with your first sense of the matter. The following guide may help you group your responses.

• Be honest with yourself. What is your *current status* in the following areas of your life:

MENTALLY _____

_____

_____

EMOTIONALLY _____

_____

_____

PHYSICALLY _____

_____

_____

SPIRITUALLY _____

_____

_____

• What aspects of your total personal health have you been ignoring? _____

_____

_____

• What aspects of your total personal health have you been dealing with? _____

_____

_____

• What results have you had? _____

_____

_____

• What aspects of your personal care need to change? _____

_____

_____

- What *positive things* are you already doing for yourself?_____
_____
_____

Spiritual markers for listening to our bodies

<u>Biblical direction</u>
- "You surely know that your body is a temple where the Holy Spirit lives. The Spirit is in you and is a gift from God. You are no longer your own. God paid a great price for you. So use your body to honor God" (1 Corinthians 6:19-20).

- "We are like clay jars in which this treasure is stored. The real power comes from God and not from us. We often suffer, but we are never crushed. Even when we don't know what to do, we never give up. In times of trouble, God is with us, and when we are knocked down, we get up again. . . . We never give up. Our bodies are gradually dying, but we ourselves are being made stronger each day" (2 Corinthians 4:7-9, 16).

- "He renews our hopes and heals our bodies" (Psalm 147:3).

<u>Action</u>
- We have the responsibility to take good care of our bodies. Our bodies do not belong to us. The Holy Spirit dwells in us, and our bodies should glorify God.

- Do not act like you are invincible.

- Let God do his work of renewal in you.

- God heals. Claim the promise!

The book of Psalms has many readings that speak to health. Other verses you may wish to contemplate are:

- I prayed to you, Lord God, and you healed me" (Psalm 30:2).

- "My body and mind may fail, but you are my strength and my choice forever" (Psalm 73:26).

- "With all my heart I praise the Lord, and with all that I am I praise his holy name! With all my heart I praise the Lord! I will never forget how kind he has been. The Lord forgives our sins, heals us when we are sick, and protects us from death" (Psalm 103:1-4*a*).

- "You created me and put me together. Make me wise enough to learn what you have commanded. . . . Let me truly respect your laws, so I won't be ashamed" (Psalm 119:73, 80).

- "You are the one who put me together inside my mother's body, and I praise you because of the wonderful way you created me. Everything you do is marvelous! Of this I have no doubt. Nothing about me is hidden from you! I was secretly woven together deep in the earth below, but with your own eyes you saw my body being formed. Even before I was born, you had written in your book everything I would do" (Psalm 139.13-16).

- "Respect and obey the Lord! This is the first step to wisdom and good sense. God will always be respected" (Psalm 111:10).

- "You bless all who depend on you for their strength and all who deeply desire to visit your temple" (Psalm 84:5).

- "With all my heart I thank you. I praise you, Lord God" (Psalm 86:12).

These verses recognize God's work in forming each one of us as a unique creation giving us life, strength and hope as living beings. We matter to God.

> "I will bless you with a future filled with hope—a future of success, not of suffering. You will turn back to me and ask for help, and I will answer your prayers. You will worship me with all your heart, and I will be with you" (Jeremiah 29:11-13).

We have examined two spiritual keys for managing stress: *taking inventory* of factors that are causing stress in our lives and *listening to our bodies*. Take some time to review your current stressors and how your body is reacting to themThe next section discusses the third spiritual key: *maintaining a balance* in the various areas of our lives.

Key 3: Maintain a balanced lifestyle

What a balanced lifestyle is not. A balanced lifestyle is not dividing our life into neat little segments of equal proportions that, in turn, allow us to experience stability and total well-being. A balanced lifestyle consists of a dynamic interplay between our mind, emotions, body, and spirit. In a balanced lifestyle we maintain a fluid passage between all areas of our life without creating an abundance in one area at the expense of a deficit in another. A balanced lifestyle for one person may not be a balanced lifestyle for another. Each individual has a different point of equilibrium. The goal is to keep our feet firmly planted on the rock of our relationship to Christ Jesus.

Contributing factors to a state of disequilibrium
By-products of the growing demands individuals experience today include over-crowded schedules, compressed time, chronic fatigue, recurring crisis, and, ultimately, being out of control. In some instances, these conditions become the norm, a way of life. If unchecked, these factors target individuals to become victims of stress secondary to the constant bombardment from pressures

of daily living. For some, this lifestyle is more a matter of existing rather than living. They master the art of going through the motions of pretense, sometimes so numb to the reality that they don't know the difference between *being* alive and *acting* alive.
Let's look at the other extreme, the lack of stimulation or involvement in life. This may be seen more often in the disengagement of elderly persons disconnected from meaningful relationships, particularly those abandoned by family and friends. This too is a state of disequilibrium. There's a lack of balance in daily living. If left unattended, the lack of meaningful involvement in life, at whatever scale, predisposes persons to fall victims to the insidious encroachment of stress.

Characteristics of a balanced lifestyle
A balanced lifestyle is a *dynamic process*. That is, it is in constant movement. It is not a static condition. As it is dynamic, it also *changes*. It flows with the needs for adaptation and survival of the individual. A balanced lifestyle makes accommodations to maintain and preserve life.
A balanced lifestyle is *inclusive*. It affects the total person: mind, emotions, body, and spirit. What happens in one area of our lives affects the other areas. There is an ongoing, active interplay between the various components of our entity.
A balanced lifestyle is *harmonious*. The distribution of energy across the various aspects of one's life is under control. One actually experiences peace with God. "Christ has made peace . . ." (Ephesians 2:14*a*). "By faith we have been made acceptable to God. And now, because of our Lord Jesus Christ, we live at peace with God" (Romans 5:1). There is peace with oneself, and with others. "Then, because you belong to Christ Jesus, God will bless you with peace that no one can completely understand. And this peace will control the way you think and feel" (Philippians 4:7). This doesn't mean that life is problem-free. However, when there is harmony within a person's life, the Holy Spirit carries out His work. "God's Spirit makes us . . . peaceful . . ." (Galatians 5:22). The person is equipped to cope, seek positive solutions, and overcome. "The LORD is my strength, the reason for my song, because he has saved me" (Exodus 15:2*a*). "You are my strong shield, and I trust you completely. You have helped me, and I will celebrate and thank you in song" (Psalm 28.7). "The LORD protects his

people, and they can come to him in times of trouble" (Psalm 37:39). "God is our mighty fortress, always ready to help in times of trouble" (Psalm 46:1).

Most importantly, a balanced lifestyle is *Christ-centered.* It is very important to recognize that a balance in life is not the result of our own strength. A balanced lifestyle is not dependent on a person's cultural identification, social position, occupation, education, denominational preference, or any other man-made criterion. Balance in life flows when we allow the Holy Spirit to dwell within us, when Christ is the center of our life, and we align ourselves with God's will. Only then can we stand firm on the rock of our salvation: Jesus Christ.

> "Can anything separate us from the love of Christ? Can trouble, suffering, and hard times, or hunger and nakedness, or danger and death? . . . In everything we have won more than a victory because of Christ who loves us. I am sure that nothing can separate us from God's love—not life or death, not angels or spirits, not the present or the future, and not powers above or powers below. Nothing in all creation can separate us from God's love for us in Christ Jesus our Lord!" (Romans 8:35,37-39).

How then do we attain and keep balance in our lives, so that we are neither overextended nor too inactive? There are several helpful action steps to consider.

Steps to a balanced lifestyle
You and I have primary responsibility for staying in touch with ourselves first. We can't depend on someone else, however loved, to establish a balance in our lives for us. This concept works like one's personal salvation. No one else can take our place. It's an individual matter. Once we accept personal responsibility for the balance in our life, then we must take inventory of our mental, emotional, physical, and spiritual condition. Is there a sense of harmony, a sense of cohesiveness in our person? Is there a disruptive pull from any part of our being? If there is a disruptive pull, where is it coming from and why? Likewise, if there is a sense of peace and well-being in one's life, what is going on to contribute

to that condition? It is helpful to take note of both conditions: the pull and the peace. Asking yourself these questions allows you to establish a base point of reference for your personal situation. Make allowances for adaptive responses to demands and to change. In other words, don't feel that something is terribly wrong in your life if you don't feel one-hundred percent well at all times. Remember that life is dynamic and changing constantly.

Once we are acquainted with our personal condition, we must assess our life experiences within the context of the family. What is family to us? Who is our family? Next to the individual, the family is another one of God's unique creations. The family is a link in a person's sense of balance in life. The family is a cradle of nurturance. A caring and loving family serves as a support net in times of distress. The family is there, too, in times of laughter and celebration. But not all is well with the family today.

Changing sociocultural conditions have thrown the family into a course of self-destruction. Stress signs are everywhere. Not only are the traditional family support systems lacking, but also intergenerational transitions are impacting the quality of life of the family. In some households, there may be as many as four generations living together. This is more common in homes of some ethnic groups, such as Hispanic American, American Indian, or Asian American. The language, values, and belief systems of the grandparents differ from those of their grandchildren. In some homes, the grandparents have not mastered the English language, so they aren't able to communicate with the grandchildren who speak only English. This creates stressful situations in the family.

In other instances, the children become the cultural "brokers" for the family because they understand English, but the parents don't. These situations also create stress for the family, because in some cultures children are to be seen but not heard. Traditionally, the children don't command the power in the family system. However, as new immigrant families, the children learn English faster then their parents and therefore become interpreters in situations where decision-making is traditionally reserved for the father. This is a growing source of social and family-based disequilibrium.

These social transitions and cultural changes in minority families are also characterized by clashes in traditional versus contemporary family values, cultural norms, and related behaviors. The older adults complain of the loss of respect for elders and for authority. The more mainstreamed the family becomes, the greater the departure from traditional lifestyles.

Sociocultural transitions in minority families also find some parents who are in the middle of the various generations attempting to bridge the gaps. Both parents have jobs outside the home. The older parents living with them need care. There are doctor appointments to make and to keep for the older persons, medications to purchase and to administer and/or monitor, as well as other needs. Depending on the fragility of the older person(s), the needs cover a wide range of responsibilities for the working couple.

Then there are their own children. In some minority cultures, it's not unusual for the children to live at home well into their twenties or thirties, if not longer. No one thinks anything about it, expect those from another cultural group who believe that something must be wrong with the child still living at home. In the sociocultural context of the minority family, sometimes the married children also live with the parents, including their own children. (An interesting contrast is the American family of European background who tends to see their offspring leave the nest at about 18 years of age.)

In the American family within the larger sociocultural context, there is a growing sense of despair. St. Clair[12] reports that every 24 hours, children and youth in the U.S. experience the following:

2,989 children see their parents get divorced.
2,556 children are born out of wedlock.
1,629 children are in adult jails.
3,288 children run away from home.
1,849 children are abused or neglected.
1,512 teenagers drop out of school.
437 children are arrested for drinking or drunken driving.
211 children are arrested for drug abuse.
2,795 teens (women under 20) get pregnant.
7,742 teenagers become sexually active.
1,106 teenagers have abortions.
1,295 teenagers give birth.
372 teenagers miscarry.
623 teenagers contract syphilis or gonorrhea.
6 teenagers commit suicide.

Because of the contemporary American lifestyle, it's reported that parents communicate with their children on average of 40 to 55 minutes per week. If we communicated likewise at the workplace with our supervisor or other coworkers, how many of us would still be employed? I venture to say few, if any. But we do that at home. We are also reaping the consequences as we see the growing rates of drug abuse, alcohol abuse, gangs, crime, violence, and suicide. Our children and youth are crying out for help. Parents are crying out for help, too. We must counteract the destructive forces of child abuse, domestic violence, and homicide. The family in America is on a roller coaster of disequilibrium and disintegration. The trend must be reversed.

There is hope for the family
I believe that there is hope for the family in America. We must begin to recover the sanctity of the family. God wants healthy families. God wants balanced families. Families matter to Him. We've taken a look at some of the pathology in the American family today. To move onward to a rediscovery of God's plan for the family, let's identify some of the signs of a healthy family. By definition, *a healthy family is a Christ-centered family.*

In health care, the diagnostician must understand what constitutes health in order to identify a deviation from health, as in the case of an illness. Only then can the health care provider develop interventions designed to help restore a person's well-being. The same is true of the family. The next chapter reveals some characteristics that are key indicators of a healthy family.

5
Vital Signs of a Healthy Family

A healthy family . . .

- **loves God.**

"But more than anything else, put God's work first and do what he wants. Then the other things will be yours as well" (Matthew 6:33).

"So love the LORD your God with all your heart, soul, and strength" (Deuteronomy 6:5).

"My family and I are going to worship and obey the LORD!" (Joshua 24:15*b*).

- **is united by a genuine love for one another.**

"But I am giving you a new command. You must love each other, just as I have loved you" (John 13:34).

- **maintains a mutual respect for one another.**

"Try to get along and live peacefully with each other. . . . (2 Corinthians 13:11*b*).

- **looks out for the well-being of each other.**

"We should think about others and not about ourselves" (1 Corinthians 10:24).

- **maintains open channels of communication.**

"The king is the friend of all who are sincere and speak with kindness" (Proverbs 22:11).

- **seeks peace and a strong faith.**

"We should try to live at peace and help each other have a strong faith" (Romans 14:19).

- **sacrifices for the well-being of the group.**

"Remember this saying, 'A few seeds make a small harvest, but a lot of seeds make a big harvest' " (2 Corinthians 9:6).

- **shares in good times and in bad times.**
"Our bodies don't have just one part. They have many parts. . . . If one part of our body hurts, we hurt all over. If one part of our body is honored, the whole body will be happy" (1 Corinthians 12:14,26).

- **provides a system of support for its members.**
"If our faith is strong, we should be patient with the Lord's followers whose faith is weak. We should try to please them instead of ourselves. We should think of their good and try to help them by doing what pleases them" (Romans 15:1-2)

- **gives without expecting something in return.**
"If a soldier forces you to carry his pack one mile, carry it two miles" (Matthew 5:41).

- **respects the privacy of its members.**
". . . try to earn the respect of others, and do your best to live at peace with everyone" (Romans 12:17*b*-18).

- **is willing to change.**
"Each of you is now a new person. You are becoming more and more like your Creator, and you will understand him better" (Colossians 3:10).

- **is willing to ask for forgiveness and to forgive.**
". . . our God, you are merciful and quick to forgive; you are loving, kind, and very patient. So you never turned away from them" (Nehemiah 9:17).

Invest in a healthy family
"Without the help of the LORD it is useless to build a home or to guard a city" (Psalm 127:1). Healthy families don't just happen. They are created. They are the result of intentional effort. Primary responsibility for developing a haven of love, acceptance, and preparation for the rest of one's life rests with the parents. Children don't come with an operations manual. Parents learn to parent by trial and error. The most effective approach to handle the daily demands of the family and to maintain a sense of normalcy is to think of family needs in terms of *challenges* and not as *problems*.

Handles for daily living

- **Know your personal strengths and limitations.**
    Successful pathways for parenting must begin with the parent as an individual. Accept yourself. If you have a problem, acknowledge it and take positive steps to resolve it. Don't wait around hoping that if you wait long enough the problem will go away. Ask for help, if necessary.
    Know what you do well. This is not limited to what you do well with your hands. It also means how you deal with attitude management, interpersonal skills, communications, being loving, and being compassionate. Take inventory.
    Learn to celebrate yourself! No one is perfect, but with God's help, you can be a better parent.

- **Be willing to change your attitudes and parental behavior in order to improve the quality of family life.**
    Don't spend a lifetime defending your actions as a parent. Instead build bridges of understanding and be willing to make adjustments that add to the well-being of the family. If you make a mistake, learn from it and move forward.

- **Make a special effort to maintain open lines of communication between everyone in the family.**
    Establish sessions for *family talks.* Set aside time to discuss problems and solutions.
    Don't be in a hurry while you are trying to communicate. Don't try to reprimand someone while you are walking out the door.
    Schedule a *special time* with your spouse.
    Schedule a *special time* with your children
    —younger and older.
    Notice body language. Don't be looking at your watch while you are talking or listening.
    Meet children at eye level.
    Model positive behavior.

- **Spend time together.**
    Prepare meals together.
    Eat together.
    Shop together.

Worship together.
Play together.
Visit family and friends together.

- **Solve problems together as a family.**
  In setting up "family talk sessions":
  - Establish the rules. For example,
    - Everyone has the opportunity to speak.
    - Avoid interruptions.
    - Withhold negative remarks.
    - Avoid being judgmental.
  - Discuss the problem.
  - Identify possible solutions.
  - Assign responsibilities to individuals for carrying out the plan
  - Don't expect to arrive at solutions every time you meet. Keep meeting until you are satisfied with the results.
  - Affirm each other.

- **Pray together as a family.**
  Prayer has a bonding effect.
  Prayer has a healing effect.
  Prayer strengthens individuals.
  Prayer strengthens the family.

- **Share love and affection with one another.**
  Verbalize your love for each other.
  Let each other know that you are there for one another.
  Use words that show consideration, like *please* and *thank you.*

- **Parents, demonstrate *unconditional love* to your children.**
  Unconditional love says:
  I appreciate you as my son.
  I appreciate you as my daughter.
  I appreciate you:
   for trying to do your very best.
   for learning to be a team player.
   for the uniqueness of who you are.

- **View parenting as a "calling" and strive to model the love of Christ.**
    "Children are a blessing and a gift from the LORD" (Psalm 127:3).
    Live a life worthy of the calling you have received. (See Ephesians 4:1.)
    Be humble and gentle.
    Be patient.
    Bear with one another in love.
    Be a peacemaker (see Matthew 5:9). It keeps the unity of the Holy Spirit.
    Speak the truth clearly and confidently based on God's Word.
    Control anger.
        "Don't get so angry that you sin. Don't go to bed angry and don't give the devil a chance" (Ephesians 4:26-27).
    Speak words that edify. Speak words that will benefit those who listen.
        "Stop all your dirty talk. Say the right thing at the right time and help others by what you say" (Ephesians 4:29).
        "Stop being bitter and angry and mad at others. Don't yell at one another or curse each other or ever be rude. Instead, be kind and merciful, and forgive others, just as God forgave you because of Christ. Do as God does. After all, you are his dear children. Let love be your guide. Christ loved us and offered his life for us as a sacrifice that pleases God" (Ephesians 4:31-5:2).

- **Keep Christ as the center of family life.**
    "My family and I are going to worship and obey the LORD!" (Joshua 24:15*b*).
    "Act like people with good sense and not like fools. These are evil times, so make every minute count" (Ephesians 5:15-16).

The children of today are the parents of tomorrow. We can

never love a child too much. Teresa A. Langston best expresses it in her verses:

A child that lives with criticism learns to condemn.
A child that lives with hostility learns to fight.
A child that lives with ridicule learns to be shy.
A child that lives with shame learns to be guilty.
A child that lives with affection learns to love.
A child that lives with tolerance learns to be patient.
A child that lives with encouragement learns confidence.
A child that lives with praise learns to appreciate.
A child that lives with fairness learns justice.
A child that lives with security learns faith.
A child that lives with approval learns to like himself/herself.
A child that lives with acceptance, learns to find love in the world.[13]

Handle it with care
Even now, as we live in these fast-paced and troubled times, the Lord still is in the business of giving hope and healing the heart. Let us rejoice in the full knowledge that God wants healthy families. Healthy families make healthy churches, and healthy churches can make a positive difference for Christ in our communities.

The family is God's creation. The family is our *first mission base*. God created the family as the first social unit. He didn't start out by creating churches or corporations. He started with a family. The family provides the foundation upon which one continues to become what God intends. The family is the cradle of nurturance for a lifetime. *Handle it with care!*

A single mother in a parenting class wrote this want ad:

WANTED
Seeking highly motivated individuals to fill full-time position. Must be willing to work 7 days a week, including all morning, evening, night, and weekend shifts for little or no pay, including no paid vacations, sick leave or holidays. Position requires that person be willing to learn on the job, be extremely patient, learn from mistakes, have good negotiating and compromising skills, as well as be a fair disciplinarian. Must

possess shopping, cooking, counseling, nurturing, teaching, bottle-feeding, diaper-changing, grooming, toileting, house cleaning, driving, musical, athletic, story-telling, CPR training, and birthday party planning skills. With a sense of humor. Must be willing to obtain a medical and/or dental certification in pediatrics. Should have a high tolerance for repetitious, annoying, high-pitched cartoon character theme songs. Must be willing to live by example. Rewards include a lifetime of endless opportunities for giving and receiving. Loving, stable, married, two-parent household a definite plus.

NOTE: *This is the most important job you will ever have!*

—Nina R. Treviño, July 1998

Commitment of love

As I've spoken about the family to various Christian groups, I've used the "Commitment of Love" pledge on the next page to strengthen family relations, beginning with the mother and father. I ask couples to participate on a voluntary basis. They face each other and repeat the words, the husband first and then the wife. If children are present, they join the parents and hug and kiss after the pledge has been said.

As simple as repeating a pledge may seem, this exercise has been revealing. In some situations, the husband has had difficulty speaking the words because it was difficult to ask for forgiveness. The same has been true for wives. As adults, we relegate asking for forgiveness to children when they disobey. We seldom think of doing the same thing ourselves. Yet, asking for forgiveness can have such a healing effect. It restores from within. It seals the open wounds.

After repeating the pledge before the congregation, couples hug and kiss. They cry. The children embrace their parents. Parents embrace the children. We may never know all that takes place during these special moments between the family members, but one thing is obvious: a sense of relief and joy.

Hold your own ceremony at home with your family. Repeat the pledge to each other. Some pastors who have participated in this exercise have used it in their churches during a worship service. You could make it an annual ceremony, an annual vow.

Share it with other families. Healthy individuals make healthy families. Healthy families make healthy churches. Healthy churches can win the lost for Christ.

COMMITMENT OF LOVE

Before God and this holy assembly
I ask you to forgive me
If I have offended you
In any way
Knowingly or unknowingly.

Today, I renew my commitment
To love you
To take care of you and our family
To respect and to honor you
For the rest of my life.

With God's help,
I commit to
Love God more
Love you more
To love our family more
So help me God.

Amen.

Dr. Margarita C. Treviño
1998

6
Establishing a Balanced Lifestyle

The best way to determine the status of your lifestyle is to take inventory. Complete the following questions and take notice honestly of where you stand with your personal situation.

- How is the balance in your life today? Do you feel you are in control of your life?

- Is there someone or something that demands a lot from you?

- How much time and energy do you set aside specifically to take care of your personal needs?

- How much time and energy are you using to take care of the needs of others?

- Do you have a balance that is healthy for you?

- Do you feel the need to make any changes? If so, in what way?

Spiritual markers for taking inventory of the balance in your lifestyle

Biblical direction	**Action**
• "Only God can save me, and I calmly wait for him" (Psalm 62:1).	• Be slient. • Wait upon the Lord • Hope in God.
• "You are my God. Show me what you want me to do, and let your gentle Spirit lead me in the right path" (Psalm 143:10).	• Ask God for direction in your life, according to His will.
• "What will you gain, if you own the whole world but destroy yourself? What would you give to get back your soul?" (Matthew 16:26).	• Take care of your personal needs first. Then you will be better prepared to take care of others.
• "Don't be jealous or proud, but be humble and consider others more important than yourselves. Care about them as much as you care about yourselves and think the same way that Christ Jesus thought . . ." (Philippians 2:3-5).	• Do not be selfish. Take an interest in others.
• "God loves you and has chosen you as his own special people. So be gentle, kind, humble, meek, and patient. Put up with each other, and forgive anyone who does you wrong, just as Christ has forgiven you" (Colossians 3:12-13).	• Be compassionate and kind. Be humble. Be gentle and have patience with others. Forgive as the Lord forgave you.

Establishing a Balanced Lifestyle

Colossians 3:14-17 emphasizes the importance of love as "what ties everything completely together." The Bible admonishes us allow the Word of God to dwell within us "while you use all your wisdom to teach and instruct each other. With thankful hearts, sing psalms, hymns, and spiritual songs to God. Whatever you say or do should be done in the name of the Lord Jesus, as you give thanks to God the Father because of him." When we obey God, we put into practice attitudes and behaviors that enable a balanced lifestyle. The Holy Spirit enables us to get rid of hindrances that could easily harm our well-being.

Keep in mind that your labor of love for yourself and others is not in vain, regardless of how difficult and stressful situations or circumstances may be in your life. Satan wants to discourage you and make you think that you are a loser, that there is no hope. Refute the enemy and claim the promises of God. "God is always fair. He will remember how you helped his people in the past and how you are still helping them. You belong to God, and he won't forget the love you have shown his people. We wish that each of you would always be eager to show how strong and lasting your hope really is. Then you would never be lazy. You would be following the example of those who had faith and were patient until God kept his promise to them" (Hebrews 6:10-12).

Pulling it all together

The National Institute of Mental Health has a leaflet called "Plain Talk About Handling Stress."[14] Examine these recommendations and choose those activities that you may find helpful. Change occurs gradually. Work on a few of the recommendations at a time.

- **Increase your physical activity.** When you are nervous, angry, or upset, release the pressure through exercise or physical activity. Running, walking, playing tennis, swimming, or working in your garden are just some of the activities you might try. Physical exercise will relieve that "uptight" feeling and relax you. Remember, the mind, body, *and spirit* work together.

- **Talk to someone.** It helps to talk to someone about your concerns and worries. A friend, family member, teacher, or counselor can help you see your problem in a different light. If you feel your problem is serious, you might seek professional help from a psychologist, psychiatrist, social worker, or mental health counselor. Knowing when to ask for help may avoid more serious problems later.

- **Recognize your limits.** If a problem is beyond your control and cannot be changed at the moment, don't fight the situation. Learn to accept what is—for now—until such time when you can change it. Focus on changing those situations that are within your power to change and accepting those situations (or people) that you cannot change.

- **Take care of your mind and your body *and your spirit*.** Get enough rest and eat well. If you are irritable and tense from lack of sleep or if you are not eating correctly, you will have less ability to deal with stressful situations. If stress repeatedly keeps you from sleeping, talk to your physician or a counselor about the problem.

- **Make more time for fun and laughter.** Schedule time for both work and recreation. Play can be just as important to your well-being as work; you need a break from your daily routine to just relax and have fun.

- **Become more of a participant.** One way to keep from getting bored, sad, and lonely is to go where it's all happening. Sitting alone can make you feel frustrated. Instead of feeling sorry for yourself, get involved and become a participant. Offer your services in neighborhood or volunteer organizations. Help yourself by helping other people. Get involved in the world and the people around you.

- **Prioritize tasks and your time.** Trying to take care of everything at once can seem overwhelming, and, as a result, you may not accomplish anything. Instead, make a list of what tasks you have to do, then do them one at a time, checking them off as they're completed.

　　Give priority to the most important ones and do those first. Ask yourself, "What is the worst possible outcome if I do not accomplish a particular task or if I eliminate it from my list?"

Establishing a Balanced Lifestyle

- **Become more cooperative.** Do other people upset you, particularly when they don't do things your way? Try cooperation instead of confrontation. It's better than fighting and always being "right." A little give-and-take on both sides will reduce the strain and make you both feel more comfortable.

- **Learn to cry.** A good cry can be a healthy way to bring relief to your anxiety, and it might even prevent a headache or other physical consequences.
  Take some deep breaths; they also release tension.

- **Dream.** Imagine a quite scene. You can't always run away, but you can dream. A quiet country scene painted mentally, or on canvas, can take you out of the turmoil of a stressful situation. Change the scene by reading a good book or playing beautiful music to create a sense of peace and tranquillity.

- **Avoid self-medication and alcohol.** Although you can use prescription or over-the-counter medications to relieve stress temporarily, they do not remove the conditions that cause the stress in the first place. Medications, in fact, may be habit-forming and also may reduce your efficiency, thus creating more stress than they take away. They should be taken only on the advice of your doctor.

- **Learn to relax.** The best strategy for avoiding the negative effects of stress is to learn how to relax. Unfortunately, many people try to relax at the same pace that they lead the rest of their lives. For a while, tune out your worries about time, productivity, and "doing right."

You will find satisfaction in just being, without striving. Find activities that give you pleasure and that are good for you, *mentally, physically, and spiritually.* Forget about always winning. Focus on relaxation, enjoyment, and health.

(The emphasis on the spiritual dimension was added.)

Meditation on God's Word as a technique for managing stress
Meditation on God's Word has a direct impact on the successful management of stress. Philippians 4:8 tells us, "Finally, my friends, keep your minds on whatever is true, pure, right, holy, friendly, and proper. Don't ever stop thinking about what is truly worthwhile and worthy of praise." Our mind is like a computer. It will put out that which is put in. If we dwell on the good and positive aspects of life, that is what our life will also reflect. Likewise, if we focus on negativity and despair, our life will reflect the same.

Hebrews 4:12-16 states,
"What God has said isn't only alive and active! It is sharper than any double-edged sword. His word can cut through our spirits and souls and through our joints and marrow, until it discovers the desires and thoughts of our hearts. Nothing is hidden from God! He sees through everything, and we will have to tell him the truth. We have a great high priest, who has gone into heaven, and he is Jesus the Son of God. That is why we must hold on to what we have said about him. Jesus understands every weakness of ours, because he was tempted in every way that we are. But he did not sin! So whenever we are in need, we should come bravely before the throne of our merciful God. There we will be treated with undeserved kindness, and we will find help."

To meditate, select a time and place in which you will have minimal distractions. Select a portion of the Bible and read consecutively, but don't try to read in assignment style. God's Word will speak to you. Meditate on the message for your heart that day and determine what action it requires from you. Pray that the Lord will enlighten you, and trust that the Holy Spirit will guide you.

Establishing a Balanced Lifestyle

Other suggestions for managing stress successfully are:
- Take a warm bubble bath.
- Go camping.
- Walk barefooted.
- Wear comfortable clothes.
- Take a nap.
- Write a note to a friend.
- Drink an herbal tea.
- Laugh.
- Sing.
- Whistle.
- Hug someone.
- Have a sense of humor.
- Sit in the patio or in the park.
- Take "mental health" breaks.
- Listen to your favorite music.
- Keep reasonable expectations of yourself.
- Keep reasonable expectations of others.
- Avoid fatigue.
- Accept the idea that it's okay to be happy.
- Accept the idea that it's okay to be sad.
- Make room for success in your life.
- Use failures as springboards to achievements.
- Be willing to give of yourself.
- Be willing to receive from others
- Be willing to lead others.
- Be willing to follow others.
- Delegate those things that others can help you do.
- Be flexible.
- Be gentle with yourself.
- Start a hobby.
- Read your old love letters you shared with your spouse.
- Go shopping.
- Read for recreation.
- Do something special for yourself.
- Plan a special time to "do nothing."

You will never stumble
"We have everything we need to live a life that pleases God. It was all given to us by God's own power, when we learned that he had invited us to share in his wonderful goodness. God made great and marvelous promises, so that his nature would become part of us. Then we could escape our evil desires and the corrupt influences of this world.

"Do your best to improve your faith. You can do this by adding goodness, understanding, self-control, patience, devotion to God, concern for others, and love. If you keep growing in this way, it will show that what you know about our Lore Jesus Christ has made your lives useful and meaningful. But if you don't grow, you are like someone who is nearsighted or blind, and you have forgotten that your past sins are forgiven.

"My friends, you must do all you can to show that God has really chosen and selected you. If you keep on doing this, you won't stumble and fall" (2 Peter 1:3-10).

The choice is yours
J. B. Phillips wrote in *Plain Christianity,* "How can you give God anything when he owns everything? But does He? How about that power to choose, that precious free will that He has given to every living personality and which He so greatly respects? That is the only present we can give—our selves, with all our powers of spirit, mind, and body, willingly, freely given because we love Him. That is the best and highest worship that you and I can offer, and I am sure that it is this above all that God most highly appreciates."[15]

Experience the *joy of victory over stress!* The choice is yours.

7
Looking Back to the Future

The Old Testament book of Jeremiah traces many of the elements common to the human experience as we still know it today. As we examine these, we find revealing parallels between Judah and modern-day Christians.

One of the commonalities is God's calling. " 'Jeremiah, I am your Creator, and before you were born, I chose you to speak for me to the nations' " (Jeremiah 1:5). As Christians, we have a common divine appointment to glorify God and to edify His Kingdom. Regardless of the particular nature of our calling as individuals, we are bonded by the commonality of divine appointment as a holy people. Jeremiah was commissioned to be a prophet "to the nations." Christians have been commissioned to "Go to the people of all nations and make them my disciples" (Matthew 28:19a).

Another common element is Jeremiah's initial response to God's call. "I replied, 'I'm not a good speaker, LORD, and I'm too young' " (Jeremiah 1:6). To this, God answered, " 'Don't say you're too young . . . If I tell you to go and speak to someone, then go! And when I tell you what to say, don't leave our a word! I promise to be with you and keep you safe, so don't be afraid.' The Lord reached out his hand, then he touched my mouth and said, 'I am giving you the words to say, and I am sending you with authority to speak to the nations for me. You will tell them of doom and destruction, and of rising and rebuilding again' " (Jeremiah 1:7-10).

Today, Christians find "reasons" not to serve God. Some claim to be unfit for the task. Others claim a lack of experience, a lack of time, a lack of money. What has God asked you to do? If you met God face to face today, how would you account for your service to Him? God isn't going to want to know the size of your bank account, or how much land you owned, or what positions and titles you had. He won't be interested in what kind of car you drove or what kind of clothes you wore or what clubs you belonged to. He won't even care about your denominational ties or what church you attended.

What God will ask you to account for as a Christian is how you used your spiritual gifts. "The Spirit has given each of us a special way of serving others" (1 Corinthians 12:7). "Each of you has been blessed with one of God's many wonderful gifts to be used in the service of others. So use your gift well" (1 Peter 4:10). God holds us accountable. . "Some time later the master of those servants returned. He called them in and asked what they had done with his money" (Matthew 25:19). Those who invested their talents wisely were rewarded. The one who did not was "thrown out into the dark where people will cry and grit their teeth in pain" (Matthew 25:30*b*). This teaches us that not only have we been chosen by God for a special work, but that God also provides us with the necessary resources to fulfill what He has called us to do. He will not assign us a mission and leave us empty-handed to try to carry it out. "You said to me, 'I will point out the road that you should follow. I will be your teacher and watch over you' " (Psalm 32:8). We don't need to be scared into serving God. We do need to know the truth.

A third commonality between biblical times and today is the prevailing social conditions. God's chosen people had forsaken Him. They had turned their backs to God. It wasn't possible to tell the difference between them and the pagan world.

> "You, my people, have sinned in two ways—you have rejected me, the source of life-giving water, and you've tried to collect water in cracked and leaking pits dug in the ground" (Jeremiah 2:13).

> "You stubborn people have rebelled and turned your backs on me" (Jeremiah 5:23).

> "You are evil, and you lie and cheat to make yourselves rich. You are powerful and prosperous, but you refuse to help the poor get the justice they deserve. You need to be punished, and so I will take revenge. Look at the terrible things going on in this country. I am shocked! Prophets give their messages

in the name of a false god, my priests don't want to serve me, and you—my own people—like it this way! But on the day of disaster, where will you turn for help?" (Jeremiah 5:27-31).

Judah was wallowing in greed, stealing, murder, lying, adultery, and deceit. They were offering sacrifices to other gods. They were worshipping the works of their own hands. Judah became a people blinded by pride. Pride was like a big, thick wall separating them from God. "Jeremiah, I will use Babylonia to destroy the pride of the people of Judah and Jerusalem" (Jeremiah 13:9).

In America, we are experiencing social, moral, and religious decline. The church has turned its back on God. Our modern-day idols are personal convenience. Quick fixes. Personal pleasure. Material possessions. Power. Prestige. Money. Computers. Technology. Information super highways. The globalization of mass communications.

The family is under siege. Parents are killing their children. Children are killing their parents. Children are killing children. As I write these pages, we have recently experienced a series of homicidal tragedies of this type across the nation. Growing numbers of families are embroiled in domestic violence. Child abuse. Alcoholism. Drugs. Teen pregnancies. Abortions. Teen suicides. We are at the top of the list of nations with the highest number of prison inmates, and the prison population continues to grow.

America has turned its back on God. Nationally, we find the country consumed by scandals in Washington. The issues have had a rippling effect throughout the world. Our attention is also turned to nuclear arms control and terrorism, here and abroad. In the meantime, growing numbers of our children are going to bed hungry. There is poverty, hunger, and destitution in America. Could it be that America, too, has more pride than humility before God?

If I had a very sick patient in Bed A and a very sick patient in Bed B, could I expect the patient in Bed A to get up and take care of the patient in Bed B? Of course not. Why? Because both of them are sick, and we can't give to someone else that which we don't have ourselves. Is it any wonder why Christians aren't reaching more unbelievers? The Church must heal from within first. We must do away with our spiritual graveyards.

Another commonality is that every decision has a consequence. It was true then, and it is true now. For the people of Judah, the consequence of her disobedience was punishment. "Listen, everyone! Some time ago, the LORD All-Powerful, the God of Israel, warned you that he would bring disaster on Jerusalem and all nearby villages. But you were stubborn and refused to listen. Now the LORD is going to bring the disaster he promised" (Jeremiah 19:15). Disaster befell Judah. They experienced famine, diseases, hunger, wars. "Warn the people of Judah that I, the LORD All-Powerful, will put an end to all their parties and wedding celebrations" (Jeremiah 16:9). "Sin pays off with death. But God's gift is eternal life given by Jesus Christ our Lord" (Romans 6:23).

The prophet Jeremiah and I share something in common. We each grew tired of living. He became depressed and simply wanted to quit. In his distress, he cursed the day he was born. "Put a curse on the day I was born! Don't bless my mother. Put a curse on the man who told my father, 'Good news! You have a son'" (Jeremiah 20:14-15). Have you ever had days like this in your life when you felt like giving up? You wondered if there were going to be any relief of your pain, your sorrow, your worry. You just wanted to quit. Your spirit was so broken that life didn't seem worth living.

Humankind knows despair. Distress is universal. We meet adversity in some form or another, at one time or another. We have two choices. We can stay Christ-centered and fight or we can flee, allowing distress to consume us. The choice is ours.

Adversity in my personal experience has had growth outcomes. While it was unclear to me as I have walked through valleys in my life, afterwards I found that the experience allowed me to know God more intimately. Subsequently, I continue to have a better understanding of my purpose in life. I continue to have a better understanding of the direction I need to take and the changes I need to make. God's love and peace continue to become more real to me.

Charles L. Allen wrote in *Roads to Radiant Living,*
"I remembered when a hurricane was headed toward Florida. The Army Air Corps wanted to make some studies of hurricanes and sent a plane out to meet this one. When they got to it, they

> flew straight into the center. It was the first time any person had ever flown into the center of a hurricane. When they got inside, they found not rain or high winds, but a perfect calm. It was so calm and peaceful that they flew around inside for some time. Later, one of those boys said that he would never be afraid of a hurricane again—if he could only get to the center of it."

Allen then compares this experience with the calming effect of expressing and ordering one's anxious thoughts. Particularly, "what so many of us need most . . . is a 'place of quiet rest, near to the heart of God.' "[16]

Jeremiah revisited his despair. "Sometimes I tell myself not to think about you, LORD, or even mention your name. But your message burns in my heart and bones, and I cannot keep silent" (Jeremiah 20:9).

"The LORD God is kind and merciful, and if you turn back to him, he will no longer turn his back on you" (2 Chronicles 30:9*b*). God's desire is that we stay close to Him. This is how we can glorify Him and edify His Kingdom. When the Pharisees told Jesus, "Teacher, make your disciples stop shouting!" (Luke 19:39*b*) because they were praising God "because of all the miracles they had seen," Jesus said, "If they keep quiet, these stones will start shouting" (Luke 19:*39b, 37, 40*).

As Jeremiah returned to fulfill his call, so we too can return to our mission field. "Pray that our LORD will make us strong and give us peace" (Psalm 29:11). We must begin with ourselves. Then our family. Next, the church. And finally, our community.

> "Can anything separate us from the love of Christ? Can trouble, suffering, and hard times, or hunger and nakedness, or danger and death? . . . In everything we have won more than a victory because of Christ who loves us. I am sure that nothing can separate us from God's love—not life or death, not angels or spirits, not the present or the future, and not powers above or powers below. Nothing in all creation can separate us from God's love for us in Christ Jesus our Lord!" (Romans 8:35,37-39).

A final commonality is God's continual call to repentance and the promise of restoration.

> "The LORD told me, 'Go to the pottery shop, and when you get there, I will tell you what to say to the people.'
> "I went there and saw the potter making clay pots on his pottery wheel. And whenever the clay would not take the shape he wanted, he would change his mind and form it into some other shape.
> "Then the LORD told me to say:
> "People of Israel, I, the LORD, have power over you, just as a potter has power over clay' "
>
> (Jeremiah 18:1-6).

God asked Jeremiah to notice what the potter was doing. The potter wasn't satisfied with the vessel he was making, so he reshaped it until it pleased his eye. If the potter, being an ordinary man, had the opportunity to redo his vessel, why shouldn't God have the opportunity to reshape His children until it pleases Him? "I will bless you with a future filled with hope—a future of success, not of suffering" (Jeremiah 29:11). " 'If you listen to me and do what I tell you, I will be your God, you will be my people, and all will go well for you' " (Jeremiah 7:23). God doesn't tire of asking us to repent that He might be our God, our Comforter, our Salvation. He calls you. He calls me. "If my own people will humbly pray and turn back to me and stop sinning, then I will answer them from heaven. I will forgive them and make their land fertile once again" (2 Chronicles 7:14).

What is your need today? Finances? Your marriage? Children or grandchildren? Work? Retirement? Health—yours or that of a loved one? Your children are leaving home for the first time—off to college, the military, getting married, moving out of the home? Are you lonely? Tired of trying alone? There is hope in the Potter's hand. Give God an opportunity to heal your hurt, to change your life, that you may find peace and rest. Your problem is not too small or too big for God. He loves you just like you are, wherever you are. Place your hand in His hand and walk the rest of the way with Him.

If you have never made a decision to accept Christ as your personal Savior, make that decision now. "God loved the people of this world so much that he gave his only Son, so that everyone who has faith in him will have eternal life and never really die" (John 3:16). "So you will be saved, if you honestly say, 'Jesus is Lord,' and if you believe with all your heart that God raised him from death" (Romans 10:9). Acknowledge that you are a sinner and that you want Christ to be Lord of your life. Give Him control of every aspect of your existence. Ask Him to forgive you. "I tell you for certain that everyone who hears my message and has faith in the one who sent me has eternal life and will never be condemned. They have already gone from death to life" (John 5:24).

Repeat these words as a statement of your desire to accept Christ as your personal Savior.

> Father God, I believe that
> Jesus Christ is your Son.
> I believe that you
> raised Him from the dead.
> I confess that I'm a sinner.
> I repent and accept
> Jesus Christ as my personal Savior.
> I want Him to be the Lord
> of my life. I pray this
> prayer in the name of Jesus.
> Amen.

If you have made the decision to follow Jesus, find a Bible-believing church and join the fellowship of other believers. They can be source of support and encouragement for you.

My personal plan

We have examined what stress is, where it comes from, how it presents itself, and how we respond to stress. I have emphasized the *spiritual response* to stress management because I believe that a spiritual orientation to stress management is the most pervasive, complete and enduring. Our final step is to develop a *personal plan* to help us remain focused in our effort to make whatever changes are indicated. Using the guide in Appendix 1, fill in the blanks. Personalize your plan. It is meant to work for you. Keep it in a place where you can see it often and continue to revise it as necessary.

Appendix 1

My Personal Plan

To improve my ability to deal with stress in my life, TODAY _____ (date), I, _____ (name), will take the following actions:

MENTALLY:

EMOTIONALLY:

PHYSICALLY:

SPIRITUALLY:

"For God has not given _____ [your name] a spirit of timidity, but of _____ and _____ and _____."

(2 Timothy 1:7 New American Standard Bible®, © The Lockman Foundation 1977).

Appendix 2

The Ultimate Benefit

The ultimate benefit of successful stress management is yours. As a healthy individual, you contribute to the making of a healthy family. The health of your family will strengthen the church where you belong. And the church where you belong will edify God's Kingdom in your community. It starts with you.

Appendix 3

The Builder

There was a man who was an efficient builder.
He had worked for years in a large company
and had reached the age of retirement.
His employer asked him to build one more house.
It was to be his last commission.

The builder took the job, but his heart was not involved
in it. He used inferior materials. The timber was poor.
He failed to see the many things that should have been
clear to him had he shown even his normal interest
in the work.

When the house was eventually finished,
his employer came to him and said,
"The house is yours. Here is the key.
It is a present from me!"

The builder immediately regretted
that he had not used the best materials
and engaged the most capable workers.
If only he had known that the house was for him!

We, as God's children, are building our own spiritual houses.
Our faithful God provides us with the best materials.
What do we use?
Let us be mindful of the many gifts of grace of our Lord.
Let us ensure that our hearts participate in everything we do.
Not one of us builds a house in eternity for someone else.
It is always for ourselves.

—*Author unknown*

Notes

Chapter 1
[1] Hans Selye, as quoted in Jerrold S. Greenberg, *Comprehensive Stress Management,* second edition (Dubuque, Iowa: Wm. C. Brown Publshers, 1987), p. 5.

[2] Greenberg, p. 5.

[3] Thomas Merton, in *The Answer*: The Holy Bible (New Century Version, © Word Publishing, 1991), "translated for our time with selected writings by leading inspirational authors" (Dallas: Word Publishing, 1993), p. 929.

[4] Ishman BodyCare Center, "The Costs of Stress." Statistics credited to "Employee Burnout: America's Newest Epidemic," Northwestern National Life; "Job Stress: The 20th Century Disease," UN International Labor Organization; and "Mitchum Report on Stress in the '90's." Online, Available: http://www.ibodycare.com/CostofStress.htm, December 1998.

[5] Ibid.

Chapter 2
[6] Questionnaire and evaluation from *Maclean's*, "Taking the Stress Test," Jan. 8, 1996, p. 36.

Chapter 4
[7] George Barna, "Today's Teens: A Generation in Transition," newsletter, p. 10; cited in Barry St. Clair, *The Magnet Effect* (Wheaton, Illinois: Victor Books, 1994), p. 15.

[8]Barry St. Clair, *The Magnet Effect* (Wheaton, Illinois: Victor Books, 1994), p. 16

[9]*USA Today*, April 17, 1990, Dobson and Bauer, *Children at Risk*, p. 207; cited in St. Clair, *The Magnet Effect*, p. 16.

[10]Greenberg, p. 5. See also: Hans Selye, *The Stress of Life*, revised edition (New York: McGraw-Hill Book Co., 1984), p. 38.

[11]Dr. Archibald D. Hart, *The Hidden Link Between Adrenalin and Stress* (Waco, Texas: Word Books, 1986), p. 32.

[12]Children's Defense Fund, Jan. 8, 1990, as cited in St. Clair, p. 17.

Chapter 5
[13]Teresa A. Langston, *Parenting Without Pressure* (Colorado Springs, Colorado: Piñon Press, NavPress Publishing Group, 1994), p. 120. Used by permission of NavPress.

Chapter 6
[14]National Institute of Mental Health, "Plain Talk About Handling Stress."

[15]J. B. Phillips, *Plain Christianity* (New York: MacMillan Co., 1954).

Chapter 7
[16]Charles L. Allen, *Roads to Radiant Living*. (Westwood, New Jersey: Fleming H. Revell Company), pp. 14-15.

Study Guide

Individual study and reflection are paramount in the application of this book. Ultimately each reader has to determine his or her own level of stress and how to handle it. Nevertheless, a group setting can be very beneficial. This could be achieved in a series of small group gatherings or in a weekend retreat. Either alternative would prove helpful to individuals wanting to achieve a more balanced lifestyle.

Retreat
The topic of stress lends itself very well to a retreat where we can get in touch with nature and be in a reflective mode. It would also probably be easier to get a guest speaker, a professional, to lead such a retreat.
   Two of the most important elements for a successful retreat are planning and promoting. Set a time and place that are attractive and convenient. Invite the speaker or speakers early, so as to allow good leader preparation. Make the book available to participants about a month ahead of time and encourage them to read it before the retreat.

Small group gatherings
Start with an introductory session to get to know each other and set the objectives of the group. Share the schedule with the participants and emphasize preparation for and participation in each session. Ask participants to commit to the following:

   Weekly Preparation
   - Read and study one chapter per week, reflecting on the content.
   - Pray that God will touch the heart of participants in the small group sessions.
   - Pray on a daily basis for the leader of the small group sessions.
   - Diligently attend each session.

Participation
- Before speaking, think about whether what you are about to say or ask will be of benefit and edification to the group.
- Do not say things that put others in a negative light.
- Allow everyone else the chance to speak as much as yourself.
- Attentively and respectfully listen to others.

Conclude this first session with a fellowship time to get to know each other better. Each week, cover one chapter in the book. Start each session with prayer. Allow most of the time for participants to share their reflections on the content. Emphasize the biblical references and ask for other Bible passages or verses the participants thought of as they read the chapter. Dismiss in prayer asking God to lead each person in a closer daily walk with Him.

One of the best things a leader can do is encourage participants to do certain activities to get the most benefit out of this study. Encourage participants to read each chapter more than once and to take time to meditate on the various parts of it and how it affects their lives. If participants speak Spanish, listening to the cassette tape version of this book will help them review and reflect on the content. Also encourage participants to choose and memorize at least one Bible verse per week that will help them handle stress better.

As you teach, appeal to different senses, especially sight. You may reproduce the graphics in this book. Perhaps you have photos, drawings, art, or music that would be appropriate to use. Think of visual object lessons for each chapter or ask participants to bring something that represents how the content applies to them. For example, for chapter three someone might bring the contents of his or her medicine cabinet and tell about how stress has led to a particular physical problem.

If you think of personal illustrations that go well with the content, use them as you teach. It will make the study warmer and fresher. This book is not exhaustive. It is a beginning place for the reader to find peace and discover God's plan for happiness and hope in our lives.

Show mercy toward the participants. Most participants will soon recognize their failures, especially in the spiritual realm. Encourage them not to waste time and energy focusing on the past, but rather to look toward the future and what they can do with their lives now.